BRINGING THE STEINER WALDORF APPROACH TO YOUR EARLY YEARS PRACTICE

Also available:

Bringing the High/Scope Approach to your Early Years Practice
Nicky Holt
978-1-84312-431-3
1-84312-431-9

Bringing the Montessori Approach to your Early Years Practice
Barbara Isaacs
978-1-84312-432-0
1-84312-432-7

Bringing the Reggio Approach to your Early Years Practice
Pat Brunton and Linda Thornton
978-1-84312-430-6
1-84312-430-0

BRINGING THE STEINER WALDORF APPROACH TO YOUR EARLY YEARS PRACTICE

Janni Nicol

Routledge
Taylor & Francis Group

LONDON AND NEW YORK

Acknowledgement
Thanks to Rosebridge Steiner Kindergarten, Cambridge and others for the photographs.

First published 2007 by Routledge
2 Park Square, Milton Park, Abingdon, Oxon OX14 4RN

Simultaneously published in the USA and Canada by Routledge
270 Madison Ave, New York, NY 10016

Routledge is an imprint of the Taylor & Francis Group, an informa business

Note: the right of Janni Nicol to be identified as the author of this work has been asserted by her in accordance with the Copyright, Designs and Patents Act 1988.

British Library Cataloguing in Publication Data
A catalogue record for this book is available from the British Library.

Library of Congress Cataloguing in Publication Data
A catalogue record has been requested.

ISBN-10: 1 84312 433 5
ISBN-13: 978 1 84312 433 7

Designed and typeset in Helvetica by FiSH Books, Enfield, Middx
Printed and bound in Great Britain by TJ International Ltd, Padstow, Cornwall

Contents

To my mother Estelle Bryer, Sally Jenkinson, Jill Taplin, Kevin Avison, Erika Grantham – and others too many to mention – for their sometimes inadvertent and unacknowledged contribution. I acknowledge you!
Without you, this book would not be possible.
With my grateful thanks.

Chapter 1
Introduction to Steiner Waldorf early childhood education

Waldorf education and early years practice today

Steiner Waldorf education is the fastest growing school movement in the world today, spanning almost every country, and keeping true to its fundamental curriculum no matter in which culture it appears, from China to South Africa, South America to Finland. The early years span pre-birth, working with parenting, baby groups and on into kindergarten (three to six years). Steiner Waldorf schools offer a real alternative to mainstream education throughout the world, and see themselves not as competitors but as partners providing a complementary provision, contributing to and learning from other educational practice. In many countries Steiner Waldorf schools are publicly funded within the maintained sector, such as Norway, Sweden, Denmark, Germany, Holland, New Zealand and Australia. In the UK there is a direct move from the Department for Education and Skills (DfES) to publicly fund Steiner schools through the Academy provision. The early years receives national funding and works with the Foundation Stage Curriculum. Teacher training is offered for all stages of the curriculum. 'Our highest endeavour must be to develop free human beings who are able to impart purpose and direction to their lives' (Steiner M., in Steiner R. 1972: 23).

Steiner Waldorf education aims to respect the essential nature of childhood, and in the early years, a secure, unhurried environment enables children to develop a range of skills which provide a sound foundation for emotional, social and cognitive intelligence later. A highly trained Steiner practitioner encourages the child's creative play and self-motivated enquiry, and offers himself or herself as example rather than instructor. Through free imitation, children naturally develop a sense of their own purposeful doing and creating alongside the working adult.

In the pre-school years the inner activities of thinking, feeling and willing are largely undifferentiated. The young child thinks in doing and expresses feelings spontaneously in word, gesture and action. At this age children learn by doing and especially by joining in with what is being done. Learning experiences are embedded within the business of daily living, and a great range of domestic and creative (artistic) activities are offered in an informal way allowing enthusiasm and initiative to flourish. The kindergarten environment provides a quality sensory experience, and is equipped with simple natural materials and toys enabling children to develop their spontaneous play, which arises from within the creativity of each child. Within the rhythmical structure of the day and week, regular activities are repeated. A sense of familiarity enables children to learn new skills without undue stress, allowing them to feel secure and confident. Opportunities for reverence, to experience awe and wonder, are developed through respect for each other and the environment. The oral tradition of storytelling, puppetry, music and movement, rhymes and songs develop memory and a rich imagination.

In the first seven years, education works with the developing children's innate rhythms in such a way that they develop a strong physical body, good motor skills, and a healthy regard and respect for each other and the world in which they live. These first seven years are a time for them to experience their childhood – in a place where they can grow in peace and harmony, feeling safe and not under pressure to perform or compete. Within this protective and homely environment a rich tapestry of essential life-learning experiences can be slowly woven, before formal teaching is introduced at seven. In Steiner Waldorf education, we call this 'place' the kindergarten.

Chapter 2

History of Steiner Waldorf education

Rudolf Steiner was born in Kraljevec, then part of Hungary, now Croatia, in 1861. He was intensely alert to nature, and was convinced of the reality of an inner life. He studied science and the classics, and tutored pupils in the humanities. Philosophy, science, literature and the arts were his principal interests, and he gained his doctorate in philosophy.

The extraordinary originality of Rudolf Steiner's mind led him to a philosophy which linked up the world of science with that of spirituality. His revolutionary ideas (called 'anthroposophy') took form in a number of enterprises, among which are art and architecture, biodynamic agriculture (organic farming working with natural rhythms), anthroposophical medicine (an extension of orthodox medical practice including Weleda medicines and toiletries), curative education and social therapy (including the Camphill movement), speech and drama, eurythmy (an art of movement making speech and music visible), Virbela flowforms (water purification systems), ethical banking and education.

The Waldorf method of education

The first Waldorf school grew out of the political and social devastation throughout Europe following the First World War. In 1919 Emil Moult, an industrialist and the founder and managing director of the Waldorf Astoria cigarette factory in Stuttgart, asked Rudolf Steiner to provide an education which could offer a healing to mankind:

> It is essential that we develop an art of education which will lead us out of the social chaos into which we have fallen. The only way out of this is to bring spirituality into the soul of human beings through education.

(Steiner 2003)

After a period of intensive teacher training, the first truly comprehensive, non-selective, non-denominational school, 'which could provide for the children of workmen and employees the same teaching and education as that enjoyed by children of families with means' (Molt 1975: 137), was founded, enabling the growth of Steiner education throughout the world. This educational impulse roused particular interest in England, where Steiner was invited to lecture in 1923. Here, he met many educationalists, forming a warm and mutually respectful friendship with Margaret McMillan – a fervent admirer.

> The need for imagination, a sense of truth and a feeling of responsibility, these are the very nerve of education... the great thing is to enable the human being to find his place in the world with due confidence in his own power of judgement.

(Steiner 1972)

Rudolf Steiner passed on his ideas for the kindergarten to Elisabeth Grunelius (1885–1989), who took on a kindergarten group for a temporary period in 1920, and then established the first Steiner kindergarten in 1926 in Stuttgart. She had worked closely with Steiner in establishing the fundamental principles for Waldorf early childhood education before his death in 1925. The school was closed by the Nazis in 1938, and in 1940 Elisabeth went to the USA, and eventually founded kindergartens there. In 1947 she returned to Germany to work with Klara Hattermann and others who were expanding the work in Europe. She gave support to teacher training and started the first international kindergarten conference in Hanover in 1951 (which continues today). Her book *Early Childhood Education and the Waldorf School Plan* was published in the USA in 1952.

Chapter 3
Steiner Waldorf early years

The kindergarten

The term 'kindergarten' originated in the nineteenth century with Friedrich Froebel. The literal translation from the German 'Kinder' and 'Garten' is 'children's garden'; 'garden' in German is connected with the word that means 'to bend' (transform, metamorphose). Froebel used this concept as inspiration for the child's environment, namely a 'paradise garden'. It is a common term for early years education in many countries throughout the world.

Children enter the kindergarten between the ages of three and six. Parent and child groups and playgroups are provided for younger children. Group sizes vary. Traditionally, five morning sessions per week are offered, each session lasting for approximately four to four and a half hours. Children take up provision according to age and need, but by five they are expected to attend five days a week. Wraparound or afternoon care is often available if required. Increasingly, providers are exploring the need for a wider early childhood provision with Steiner Waldorf nurseries and all-day kindergartens, and the move to the children centre concept; combining health, care and education, involving specifically working with parents, is a concept particularly compatible with Steiner education.

General educational principles

The seven-year periods

Steiner divided the broad principles of child development, and the educational methodology supporting it, into three psychological and physiological phases of childhood, each approximately seven years in length. These indicate a change, both physically and mentally, around the ages of 6 to 7 years, the second period including puberty to 14 years and with the development to adulthood culminating around 21 years old. Although each stage has a precise integrity, processes coming to a certain culmination in one phase transform into faculties in the subsequent stage of development. An example of this is that the forces so strongly at work in building up the physical body in the first seven years become available as the basis for healthy cognitive development later on. This threefold approach involves a holistic support for the development of the all-round human qualities of willing (doing), feeling (emotions) and thinking (semantic, affective and cognitive) – in truth an education of hand, heart and head.

The first seven years

Social, emotional, cognitive, linguistic and physical skills are accorded equal value in Steiner Waldorf early childhood education and many different competences are developed. Activities reflect the concerns, interests and developmental stages of the child and the carefully structured environment is designed to foster both personal and social learning. The curriculum is adapted to the child and takes as its starting point the careful observation of the nature of the growing and evolving human being seen in his or her physiological, psychological and spiritual aspects. It looks at the inner nature of the child, rather than theoretical or ideological aspects.

This view that the physical, emotional and cognitive/intellectual development are subtly and inextricably linked underpins and informs the early childhood curriculum, which is tailored to meet the child's changing needs during each phase.

Developmental stages

At each developmental stage, the child presents a particular set of physical, emotional and intellectual characteristics which require a particular (empathetic) educational response in return. This is the basis of a child-centred education. The formative period before second dentition (five to six years) is seen as the period of greatest physical growth and development. Structures in the brain are being refined and elaborated, a process which is not completed until after the change of teeth, and until that time the young child's primary mode of learning is through doing and experiencing – he or she 'thinks' with the entire physical being.

Early learning

The nature of this early learning should be self-motivated, allowing the child to come to know the world in the way most appropriate to his or her age – through active feeling, touching, exploring and imitating, in other words, through doing. Only when new capabilities appear, at around the seventh year, is the child physically, emotionally and intellectually ready for formal instruction. Through experiential, self-motivated physical activity the small child 'grasps' the world in order to understand it – a prerequisite for the later activity of grasping the world through concepts. Children are encouraged to master physical skills before abstract intellectual ones.

Formative forces

The core idea relevant for the first seven years is that the formative forces (those working on the development of the physical body, the brain and nervous system, in the sense organs, in walking and motor co-ordination, in linguistic development and the establishing of behaviour patterns) are emancipated in and around the seventh year and become available for other developmental processes. At the end of this phase of development, these formative processes become active differentiation of thinking, feeling and willing. This is particularly apparent in the development of cognitive and intellectual abilities. The child becomes able to increasingly direct and focus attention for longer periods of time, an ability essential to the challenges of formal learning. This is accompanied by the increasing ability to form active mental images at will, an ability vital to the mastering of abstraction such as is needed for the conceptual activities associated with reading, writing and mathematics.

It is a primary principle of Steiner Waldorf education that formal education is only introduced with the transformation of these formative forces. The premature engagement of such forces in early intellectual learning can lead to the weakening of the physical forces of regeneration and possibly also a tendency to certain learning difficulties. These days young children are exposed to many influences that weaken their constitution and prematurely call upon their formative forces and vitality. The extra stress of early formal and academic learning can seriously undermine their overall development and well-being. Steiner Waldorf education sees the establishment of the seven-year rhythm as an important cultural pedagogical task, one that can help children strengthen their inner forces and harmonise their development.

Imitation and example as an educational approach and aid to the healthy development and engagement of the will of the child

The kindergarten is a community of 'doers' supported through meaningful work, for example by baking bread or working in the garden. The children are welcome, but not required to help. The activity of the teacher may inspire the children to become independently active, finding their own learning situations in play. Children perceive and register everything the adults do – it is not only what one does before the young child but also how one does it. Teachers are conscious of their own moral influence upon the child and of the development of good habits through imitation:

> before the second dentition [the child lived mainly] in the region of the will, which was intimately connected with the child's imitating its surroundings. But what at that time entered the child's being quite physically, also contained moral and spiritual forces that became firmly established in the child's organism.

(Steiner 1972: 116)

This means that the will of the child can be developed and become strong through good habits, consequences and limits set by the adult as his or her example.

Working with the will

Working with the will takes two forms: the child's will is **activated** by the image of the adult engaged in activity and **engaged** by the purposeful work of the adult. When the adult is involved in his or her own work, (usually domestic) this creates an environment which is already active. The child is totally free either to join this activity or task and work from imitation following the adult's example, or, by being left in this already creative and active environment, to become involved in play. Here one can establish an orderliness, rhythm and good habits that belong to the 'right' physical environment. Imitation is will activity. You cannot teach imitation, it has to be done with one's own will.

There was a five-year-old girl in my kindergarten who each time she did a drawing, perhaps only one a day, rolled it into a scroll and tied it with a piece of wool to take home to Mum. After a few weeks of wrapping, rolling and tying all sorts of knots, she asked to be shown how to tie a bow. For the next few days, all she did was tie up pieces of paper, 'making presents for all her friends', she said, but it was the tying of the bows which was the driving force. She did not join in any play, but just sat at the table tying and tying these parcels. Once she had mastered the bow tying, she lost interest and went on to play with friends, as if this had never happened.

Will activity is very individual, and we can observe this in the different ways children imitate. For example, everyone has the same thing in front of them, but their reactions are quite different. Some children immediately start to imitate, or to play nearby the adult, taking in the atmosphere of the working activity, while other children don't get the impulse at all. Within imitation there is freedom.

We engage the child in a natural way when we are, as adults, involved in 'meaningful' activities worthy of imitation, tasks which have a purpose and an end product that enhance the well-being of others and ourselves. Where possible these tasks should also be completed and not left half done. Taking part in any activity helps with learning, and technology is used which is incidental and integral to the activity: real woodwork equipment, grinders and blenders, scales for weighing, weaving looms, cookers for baking and cooking etc.

The activities which we do in the kindergarten are divided into two areas: domestic and artistic.

Domestic activities

These enhance the physical body. They contain archetypal movements and activity, much of which is lost today. Making the bread, the physical act of kneading the dough, brings it alive – the ingredients, feel and outcome, the taste, texture and sheer enjoyment! Here, bread baking becomes an activity which is both educational and worthy of imitation, and also engages the will. The children work through the process of first planting the grains of wheat, watching and cultivating the growing wheat, harvesting, winnowing, threshing, grinding it, and adding the ground flour to the flour with which they bake. They weigh, measure, count, stir, watch the yeast rise and mix the dough. They knead it, bake it and finally eat it. A whole process.

This process is repeated weekly, on the same day, and this weekly rhythm and repetition of this activity also works to harmonise those active will forces.

Another example of engaging the will in domestic activity could be sweeping. This also raises questions: Where does the dust come from? Where does it go? There is a beginning and an end, which is satisfying to

the child, and a harmony in the archetypal movements. Scrubbing and cleaning the table before eating is something we all do. Washing, mending, cooking, decorating, gardening, tidying – these are domestic tasks worthy of imitation because they have a positive outcome and are on a level the children can understand. They are good for the well-being of the physical body – the child re-enacts reality until the skill is acquired, becoming good citizens in the process.

These activities are also important in the home; the child has the opportunity to clean and tidy (even if it does take forever). It is the process that is important, not necessarily the outcome, and these are life skills which enable us to contribute not only to our own self-development, but also to society and the earth.

Artistic activities

Artistic impulses come from within the child, enhancing creativity and enriching inner life. The activities that result from these impulses are painting, drawing, modelling and crafts such as weaving, woodwork, sewing etc. Singing, music and stories feed the inner life by allowing the child to create mental pictures, using imaginative faculties. All of these artistic creative activities which the child undertakes are free to come from inner creativity. Anyone watching the child involved in an artistic activity is amazed at the capacity for involvement and creativity from will activity.

- ■ **Crafts** which the children make as part of these activities are usually seasonal, and are generally made with equipment found in nature. Sheep's wool – washed, dyed and carded – can be spun, woven and felted. Tissue paper is used to make birds, butterflies, flowers and other decorations. Lanterns are made for the Martinmas festival, and at Christmas the children make presents and decorations for their families and home, sewn or sometimes made out of wood or other materials. The crafts and creativity are endless.

- ■ **Painting** is done in a particular way. It is called simply 'wet-on-wet' painting. Good quality paper is soaked in water, and sponge dried onto a large board. Diluted watercolour paints are used in the three primary colours, and these are placed on the table with a jar of water and a sponge for wiping the brush. The children sing a painting song before beginning, and the mood is always peaceful. The paintbrushes are an inch wide and quite long, and the children 'stroke them like a pussycat', imitating the teacher as he or she paints with them. As the paper and the paints are wet, the colours run into each other, and the children are delighted to discover that they have made the secondary colours as they mix together. Red and blue make purple, red and yellow make orange, yellow and blue make green and altogether they make ... mud! The children wash their brushes in the water and dry them on the sponge before putting them into the next colour, and when finished, they carry their paintings boards to the rack to dry. With painting in particular, it is the process which is important, not the outcome.

■ **Drawing material** is accessible at all times, and drawing as a joint activity sometimes takes place. The teacher draws with the children, using good paper on a drawing pad, and block crayons made from beeswax and plant colours. Black is not used. The children sometimes imitate each other and at times they draw part of a told story, or a seasonal picture, but usually freely from themselves. They are encouraged to 'finish' the picture by covering the whole paper, and to use the other side if they want to continue. Using these particular crayons, which are particular to Steiner equipment, promote the use of good pencil holding when using the tips for fine drawings, and the flat areas mix the colours together and cover the paper easily.

Implicit learning

During the early years, teaching is by example rather than by instruction or direction, relying on the child's innate power to imitate. Understanding the imitative nature of the young child is the key to teaching and discipline. Learning is 'caught rather than taught', in other words the emphasis is on implicit informal rather than explicit formal learning. Children learn through participation and imitation in the meaningful context of the rhythms of the seasons and the daily activities within the framework of the week. This approach distinguishes itself from formal learning in which the child is aware he or she has to learn. Progressions are planned and live in the consciousness of the teacher but are not explicit. The older children are expected to accomplish tasks which are explicit. Obviously there are many transitions from informal to formal learning.

Providing the child with a positive model to imitate means that all the actions, deeds and even thoughts, should be worthy of imitation by the young child: 'Imitation is the activity of the will. The activity of the will is the activity of the "I", the ego. The greatest freedom lies in imitation' (Jaffke 2002: 73).

The child's whole body is a sensory organ uniting external impressions with the internal world – similar to the function of the eyes. Eyes themselves do not see but act as mediators through which we see. Everything we absorb, therefore, reflects on the development of the child: physical, social, psychological and organic. Every perception is first deeply assimilated, then grasped with the will and reflected back in echo-like activity. This interaction of external impressions with the child's internal organic development is revealed in the wonderful power of imitation with which every healthy child is born.

Important priorities therefore arise for educators and parents (parents are the child's first educators) in selecting or filtering impressions which confront the child, and providing impressions which are worthy of imitation. To provide this protection we need to be aware of the effects of impressions:

- physical – suitable clothing, touch

- emotional and behavioural – arguing, shouting, emotional tension, physical behaviour

- sensory – as far as possible, to select the impressions which confront the child such as those from television, radio, music, traffic.

Is what they are confronted with in daily life what we want them to imitate, absorb and to become?

From a pedagogical point of view if we are aware of the child's innate power of imitation, it requires that we become good role models encouraging the right impulses through our actions. We can become aware of our behaviour, how we apply ourselves to our work in the home or garden – in the way we take care of and speak to each other, in the way we develop and care for our environment. Anyone interacting with the child becomes part of the educational process of that child.

Phases of imitation in development

In the first six to seven years the imitative behaviour of the child passes through three distinct phases, connected with the forces of organic development which influence the whole body.

■ **First stage: 1 to 2.5 years**
   During this time children acquire three of the most important human abilities:
   ☐ to stand upright and walk
   ☐ to speak
   ☐ to think in words.

They do this only through imitation (children deprived of human contact do not acquire these human abilities in a normal way). During this period the child uses will forces unconsciously, and everything is done simply out of imitation and habit without reflection or consideration. What children observe determines how these habits develop, and at the same time, they will experience how far they can go. If the adult picks the rattle up off the floor when the child throws it from the high chair, the child will automatically do it again and again, seeking the adult's attention. It is so important to provide simple toys at this stage; natural organic forms such as wooden logs, shells, conkers etc. which will stimulate them (see Chapter 4). Toys with mathematical fixed forms, or which are complete in themselves, do not stimulate the child's formative and imaginative forces.

■ **Second stage: 3 to 5 years**
   Around this age, two new faculties develop: imagination and memory. Children begin to use things around them in a different way, transforming and creating with the objects each time in a new way; what was previously a round slice off a log, now becomes a wheel or a plate. What they observe from their surroundings is now imitated in their play:

As the muscles of the hand grow firm and strong in
performing the work for which they are fitted, so the
brain and other organs are guided into the right lines of
development if they receive the right impressions from
the environment.

(Steiner 1996b: 25)

Third stage: 5 to 7 years

The forces of development most at work during this time are those
which drive the child into self-initiated activity – the 'will forces'. At
around the age of five, children experience what could be called an
'inner boredom', as if they have been abandoned by their imagination,
and often the cry of 'I don't know what to do!' is heard.

Children begin to lose that innate imitative power, and their thinking
emerges in a more conscious way; it now becomes important to
encourage them to participate more in adult activities: cleaning,
washing, sweeping, cooking, sewing, woodwork. Then transformation
takes place and children begin to play from an inner picture, as a pre-
conceived image. They plan their play and it becomes more organised.

It is really important therefore to create spaces which allow a child to
play creatively and provide the opportunity for imitation. The outside
world is observed and reflected in the play of children, who then re-
enact this observation over and over until the skill is acquired. This can
also work in a negative way if they are exposed to negative behaviour
or to violence in their surroundings or media, to swearing or other
aggressive behaviour. In the kindergarten it is all too often played out
in some form, sometimes re-enacted in order to understand it or
experience it themselves, or sometimes simply to work it out of their
systems. For instance, one can often see the whole kindergarten
moved around during the free play time when a child has moved
home!

A picture of the development of the will forces is clear in this description,
from Joan Almon a kindergarten teacher from the USA:

A six-year-old boy who built himself a car in the
kindergarten was now trying to find a way to steer it. The
car was made of two stumps of wood which had been
turned on their side with a wide board lying across them.
If he straddled the board and pushed with his feet, he

could make the car roll a bit, but he could not steer it this way. On this particular day he wanted to find a way to steer it and spent 45 minutes trying to tie a rope onto the stumps and onto the board in such a way as to connect the two and manoeuvre it. Again and again he tried it, first one way and then another. At last he gave up, and with a shrug dropped his rope and went off to play with a friend. One felt he had learned as much from a seeming failure as he would have from a success. One day he would realise that an axle and a drive shaft are needed for this step, which a simple rope could not accomplish. In the meantime, he had fully directed his will to the task and seemed not at all frustrated by his inability to make it work.

In the kindergarten, opportunity is provided for children to play out their observations by allowing time for child-initiated play with simple materials which can be adapted using their fantasy and imagination, and it is best achieved by the presence of adults purposefully occupied, where children can be 'securely enveloped' by adults' work. The adult thus occupied provides a rhythmical and ordered structure, demonstrating an enjoyment of work as well as the willingness to work hard. However, as you can see in the next chapter, the teacher has plenty of opportunity to guide this play should it be required.

Chapter 4

Play as the serious work of childhood

Play embraces children's total experience. They use it to tell their stories; to be funny and silly; to challenge the world; to imitate it; to engage with it; to discover and understand it; and to be social. They also use play to explore their inmost feelings. In a single game – playing alone or with friends – the child can switch play modes, one minute imitating the television, the next making a discovery which leads to new thinking, then being reminded of something else and changing the play accordingly, and suddenly being swamped by feelings, which require their own corresponding set of images, propelling the game in yet another direction. Like dreams, play is not ordered and rational. It does not give priority to one kind of experience or one kind of knowledge over another.

(Jenkinson 2002: 42)

The *Start Right* document on nursery education (Ball 1994) laid down that 'play is the serious work of childhood'. In a time when play is regarded as any pre-prepared activity used as a learning tool to predetermine an outcome (the 'learn as you play' model), Steiner education takes the view that this deprives the child of the freshness and nourishment of freely chosen, open-ended play, that really creative play is unpredictable and has endless outcomes.

Children still live in a dreamy world full of feeling and their own feelings are still unconscious, which is why they can imitate. Through this imitation of the world around them they can learn from life. The play is thus continually moving and creative, and with endless educational content. The following is an example of this open-ended play from my kindergarten in Cambridge:

Ike had built a van. He was a builder. There were two seats in the van and the children were keen to join him. Owen got his tools and shared the driving. They had piled up chairs to sit on (vans are higher than cars) and the front of the van was a bent screen across which they had balanced a plank, the steering wheel (a slice of round log) was placed on it, and there was a brake, accelerator etc. made of wooden blocks. Ami wanted a ride to the safari park, and kindly Owen made space for her. They 'drove' this van to the park, and then needed binoculars to see the animals. Ike and Ami fetched paper and string, and made binoculars which they took back to the van, which Owen had been looking after. By this time, other children, interested in the play, had joined them. Owen directed them into becoming animals in the park, and they had to build pens to keep them separate. Another child decided to feed the animals, and put conkers into bowls, pushing the bowls with care under the screens which 'penned' the animals.

This play lasted for around an hour, continually growing and changing as children joined, and during this time the adults sat at the table preparing the snack and observing. There was no need to interfere, guide or lead this play in any direction, as the teachers' work is to observe the children and the play, not to continually interrupt to ask questions or 'tick' responses; the creative process is interfered with as little as possible. In socio-dramatic play:

> Children who show the greatest capacities for social make-believe play also display more imagination and have less aggression. They also have a greater ability to use language for speaking and understanding others, show more empathy and are able to see things from the perspective of the other; and show less signs of fear, sadness and fatigue.

(Klugman and Smilansky 1990: 35)

There are many different forms of play:

- socio-dramatic play
- solitary play
- exploratory play

- play involving leaders and followers
- play which follows a 'script' (e.g. TV show)
- re-enactment of stories
- animal play
- floor play
- outside play.

So what do children gain from creative play?

- They learn to negotiate.
- They learn to change ideas.
- They learn to develop relationships and emotional responses.
- They learn to deal with success and failure.
- They learn to improvise.
- They learn to create anew.
- They learn to consolidate their ability to understand and think.
- They learn to develop concentration.
- It supports physical, emotional and social development.
- It strengthens imagination.
- They learn through investigation, exploration and discovery.
- It encourages inventiveness and adaptability.
- They learn how to solve problems.
- They learn practical skills.
- They learn to use self-control.
- They learn to share and take on the perspective of others.
- It develops language and communication skills.

Gordon Sturrock, said:

> **Playing has at its core a powerful adaptive functionality linked to human growth and development. The simple cue and response – the play cycles of the playing child –**

mirror the process of evolution itself. In the frames of their play, children create themes and motifs, which reflect and re-order their understanding of the world as it is and as they will go on to create it.

(Sturrock 2005)

Play requires both imagination and fantasy, the very foundations of flexibility and creativity which also promote self-confidence and self-esteem. During the kindergarten morning the time for free play is therefore given priority (both inside and out).

Play and child development

Adults reflect through discussion, through literature, through writing and meditation. Children reflect through concretely acting out past experiences, or concretely preparing for them.

(Bruce 2003)

Children under three play realistically; they imitate the world around them. They have to find out what the earth is made of, how it works, who are the people in it, how do they work. They need the involvement of adults to imitate, or to play with, and are involved with the activities of the mother, father or others around them. They play repetitively, building the brick tower and knocking it down again and again, with joy each time, before moving on to the next thing, and interact enthusiastically with their surroundings, finding each experience fresh and exciting. They only begin to socialise and interact directly with other children around the age of three. Until then they tend to play alongside, involved intensely in their own individual experiences. I remember my daughter's favourite plaything at this age was emptying and sorting the container cupboard while I was busy in the kitchen – piling up the empty storage tubs, finding the lids which fitted, banging them with a wooden spoon and only putting them back when I made a game with her of stacking them back into the cupboard.

Between the ages of three and five the children's ideas and imagination are triggered first by the object or toy and then by some memory which brings the object into play. A footstool could be a table set for a tea party to which a friend would be invited, and shortly after could become a doll's bed when upturned and filled with a cushion – time for a nap after tea! In order to play in this way, children need to have experienced these things already, and so recreate them in play. Play is now stimulated by external events, and this is why it is important that there are toys or objects available to the children that can be transformed by them into anything they wish it to be. That cut-off slice of round log could become a tray, a plate, a steering wheel, a computer keyboard – or a log to build with! (See section below on toys and playthings.) Now play is more social, children interact and need each other to transform and mould the play. They are stimulated by each other's ideas and experiences. They begin to negotiate, learn boundaries and limitations, investigate possibilities, build their language and communication skills and hopefully learn to empathise and care for each other. They play with increased concentration, but the play can still result in chaos, and often needs intervention or direction from the adult, a guiding hand to extend the play or help with social interaction.

Being involved with the domestic activities in the kindergarten also stimulates play at this age, and joining the adult with the washing of the doll's clothes, for instance, often leads to extended play, in creating the right place to hang the washing by stringing lines across the garden, fetching washing baskets to hang it up, and building a little house nearby with screens and muslins to extend the 'home' play. This could (and has in my kindergarten) led to all the children becoming involved in the process of doing the washing, hanging it up, making ironing boards out of planks with wooden blocks as irons, dressing the dolls, cooking the dinner and generally involving all and sundry in household activities.

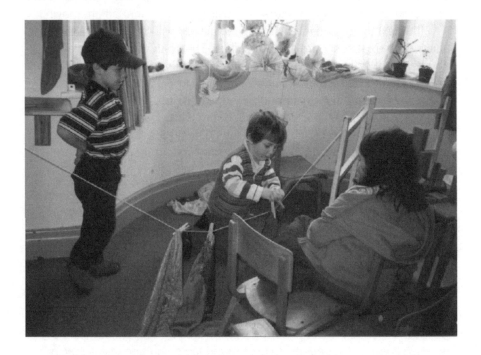

Around or after the age of five the play begins to change. Many children experience what could be called 'boredom'; they often say 'I don't know what to do'. It is as if they have been abandoned by their imagination and fantasy, and have no ideas left. This is the time where they can be stimulated directly by the adult work. They should be encouraged to join in with the work in the kindergarten, cutting up the vegetables and fruit, having tasks such as sewing, weaving or woodwork – always tasks which need to be completed. It does not take long for this phase to pass; it could be hours or a few days before new ideas for play arise naturally, and the transformation from one type of play to another takes place.

Now the initial idea comes first, followed by the attempt to find the right materials. They have this mental image of what they want to do or be. For instance, before the age of five, the child sees a stick, picks it up and begins to play at being knights, with the stick as a sword. After around the age of five he or she says 'I would like to be a knight, and I need a sword' and then looks around for wood to make one, and generally it needs to look right! The child has a mental image of what the sword should look like, and could spend hours sawing, hammering and sanding this sword until it looks good enough to play with. The impulse goes from being stimulated by the object or toy, which leads to the play, to the idea for the play, then looking for the toy or object to support it. The imagination is set to work again!

Readiness for formal learning

Readiness for more formal education is a measure of a child's abilities as a whole developing human being, what Steiner referred to when he spoke about the three foldness of the human being. One-sided development can only leave other sides undeveloped. Only when a child is

- physically/bodily ready (ideally robust, co-ordinated, secure)
- mentally ready (ideally able to begin to think in self-generated mental pictures and sequences)
- socially and linguistically ready (ideally able to learn in a group, and to communicate needs)
- spiritually ready (ideally able to begin to learn out of authority)

can we really speak of readiness for formal education. In most cases children are not ready in this holistic sense before they are six years old. Therefore they spend this last year in the kindergarten working on developing skills needed for the next stage.

During this last year in the kindergarten, the educators work more with the will forces of the child. It is important that the children complete the tasks that they begin, that they begin to take responsibility for themselves, their actions and for others. The children have tasks which contribute to the well-being of themselves and of others, and of the world around them. They tidy, clean, sweep, decorate, cook, take care of plants and animals, serve others, run messages, help the 'little ones' and develop skills and co-ordination which will help them later on. Their craft work takes on a different dimension. They may complete a 'handwork bag' for big school, designing and sewing it. They may make their own knotted doll, and weave a blanket to wrap it in, or make a wooden puppet or boat. All of these skills develop hand–eye co-ordination, small and large motor skills, concentration, and an ability to follow and understand instructions. They can transform the mental image which arises through words into their own activity.

During play, the children now need clearly defined limits and clear directions, such as 'we don't shoot each other in our kindergarten' or 'that play is not suitable for inside, please wait until we go outside'. This sets limits and boundaries for children, which are quite suitable to their age. Further directions can also be given now to extend their play, such as 'why don't you fetch some paper and a stick and make a flag for the top of your castle?' As an example from my kindergarten, some children had built a boat. The older boys were beginning to get a bit rowdy, and the younger children, who were passengers and sitting quietly fishing from the side, became upset at the noise. I suggested to one of them that they may need a basket to collect the fish from the fishermen. This led to some rope making (twisting wool together to make ropes), and then the children built an extensive contraption with the ropes and some baskets, using hoists and levers, poles and planks to wind the baskets out of the water. This extended the play, not only to at least an hour that morning, but throughout the rest of the week, changing and growing all the time. Sally Jenkinson puts it so aptly:

> There are precious few places where children can freely develop their own culture, and where the creative spirit of childhood can perform its magical transformations...
> A Steiner Waldorf Kindergarten tries to be such a place; a place where the echoing voices of children at play can still be heard.

(Jenkinson 1997: 48)

Play today

It can no longer be taken for granted that all children can play with spontaneity, fulfilment and enthusiasm appropriate for their stage of development. This is due to the influences to which they are subjected; for example, electronic gadgetry, TV, the media and ready-made technically sophisticated toys leave behind a feeling of emptiness and a demand for more. Saturation entertainment has taken over the playtime and home life of children. Sally Jenkinson gives an example:

A mother once told me how her child had once played a game of postman. The slatted back of a dining chair became his post box; he made his own letters and tiny stamps, (complete with queen's head), borrowed a hat and cloak, made himself a silver foil badge and played at delivering letters to various destinations around his house for hours. A kind aunt, having seen his obvious delight in the game whilst visiting, later bought him a manufactured toy postman set from the shops. He never played with it. The charm of his own play lay in his creative participation and in his ability to transform; each little invention brought its own pleasure and allowed the child to add something of himself to the game.

(Jenkinson 1997: 47)

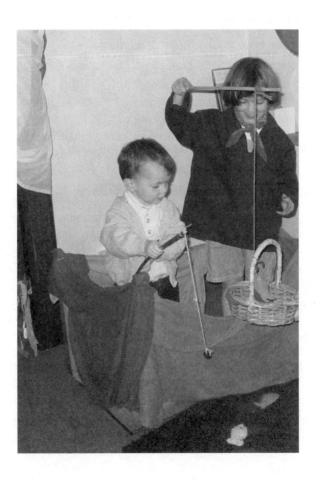

Toys and playthings

Play is stimulated by external circumstances, so objects the children play with should not be complete and should be able to be transformed by them. Visitors to a Steiner kindergarten are always surprised at what they see as a 'lack' of playthings for the children. There are certain considerations, however, which are taken into account when choosing toys for the children:

■ that they stimulate the imagination and fantasy by being whatever the child wants them to be

■ that they appeal to the senses, by being made from natural materials in soft colours

■ that they are 'collectable' from nature, e.g. sea shells, pebbles, pine cones

■ that they enable the children to create anew each time – a fresh invention

■ that they are not electronic or programmable

■ that they are repairable where possible

■ that they can be home made

■ that they represent items found in the home

■ that they are as simple and beautiful as possible.

Some suggested toys in the kindergarten

■ **Baskets** containing pine cones (trees for floor play or puppet shows, food or kindling for a pretend fire) pebbles of all sizes (for sorting, making patterns, floor play or food), bean bags, conkers, clothes pegs, bark, feathers, shaped wood for building bricks, wool (for tying, rope making, weaving), carded or washed and dyed sheep's wool in different colours, play-cloths such as lengths (half-metre to metres) of dyed muslin (for making walls, houses, dressing up, wrapping dolls), silk, cotton, wool etc.

■ **Building:** wooden planks of different lengths with slightly rounded corners, large logs cut into slices and large building blocks; low boxes, stools, carpets and tables for building on; clothes stands (fold-out, such as old washing stands, or purpose built to act as houses, shops, puppet theatres).

- **Dressing-up clothes:** different materials to act as saris, dresses, fairy wings, cloaks, crowns, hats, scarves, bags.

- **Home corner:** containing tables, stools and chairs, kitchen equipment (cooker etc.), spoons, scoops, baskets, crockery and cutlery, doll's beds or hammocks including bedding, cushions, lengths of material, baskets for shopping etc.

- **Hobby horses, prams.**

- **Dolls:** the doll is considered one of the most important toys for children of all ages. It is the image of a human being and is therefore important to develop the self-image of the child. In the kindergarten the dolls are not complete in all anatomical details or technically perfect, but made in such a way as to enable the children to use their imagination so that the doll can embody every possible view of the human being.
  - The **knotted doll** is the first, one which many children make for themselves in their last year of kindergarten. It is made by knotting a piece of flannelette into head and arms, leaving the rest loose, then hemmed. The eyes and mouth are simply marked with crayon.
  - The **formed doll** is the most common doll used in the kindergarten, and this too is made simply from stuffed fabric, soft and cuddly, with woollen hair which can be plaited or tied up, and eyes and mouth sewn in a neutral expression – children can imagine the smile, the frown, the tears or the joy according to their mood. The dolls are dressed, swaddled, taken for rides in the pram, put to bed, 'fed' or cared for as a mother would her own child.

- **Floor or table top:** small, wooden, simple animals and families able to stand; puppets, knitted or sewn animals; carts and boats; curved wood used for houses or bridges; houses carved from logs; wheeled toys made from small logs or carved wood cars.

- **Outside toys** consist of large building materials, sticks and branches, logs and planks (for making see-saws or slides, tents and tepees), collections of shells, pebbles etc. as before. Digging equipment is important for gardening or sandpit play. Rope ladders, climbing equipment, trees and ropes for building, hoops and skipping ropes, stilts and horse harnesses, and some rolling equipment such as wooden carts, wheelbarrows and so on. We do not use bikes or scooters as they cannot be used imaginatively for construction.

Chapter 5

Providing a safe, child-friendly environment

The entrance lobby

The entrance to the kindergarten room is warm, welcoming and parent-friendly. You will find child-height coat pegs, and a bench under which there is a shelf for slippers and shoes and wellington boots (unless they are kept in a separate place near the outside door with the wet weather gear). There is usually a parents' notice board, indications of what is happening in the kindergarten that week, a diary and some photographs. The festivals and events are often displayed outside the room as well. There is often a library and school shop, fresh flowers and seasonal displays, as well as a parents' helping rota. (Parents are expected to participate in the life of the kindergarten, including the cleaning, washing up and occasionally taking the washing home.)

The kindergarten room

This should be a warm, welcoming and artistically decorated space which serves as the setting for what the day's impulse brings. It is often described as a 'home from home' and should reflect the home as much as possible. Many kindergarten staff like to have the kitchen area as integral to the room, and this usually contains a small cooker, kettle, toaster, sink and washing and preparing facilities. The kitchen area is separated from the main room by the work surface and a small gate which prevents access by the children. They can on a special box step at the outside of the preparation work area and reach the sink. Furniture is small scale and child-friendly; tables and chairs for activities are nearby. These are all made of wood. There is a home play corner, a quiet area (with in some cases a few select picture books) and the play area with carpet (big enough for the ring time circle).

The room is painted (usually colour washed) in a pale pink (Rudolf Steiner described it as peach blossom pink) and is only decorated with seasonal branches and mobiles. Corners are sometimes softened with hanging muslins as well. The windows are curtained with pink dyed muslins, and the electric lighting, if used at all, is subdued. The whole impression is one of a calm, uncluttered and peaceful environment. There are no displays of children's work on the walls although at times if the children have been busy with a seasonal craft, it is hanging in some area of the room. For example spider's web weaving, birds at Whitsun, Valentine hearts, tissue paper butterflies and felted chicks. All of these add to the seasonal feel of the room, and are taken home at the appropriate time.

The seasonal table

This is placed in a position within the room where it is visible and central, and yet unobtrusive. The seasonal table is a place where treasures are displayed and woven together with elements of the season's mood. It develops and changes throughout the year to reflect the changing festivals or seasons. The colours are dictated by the colours in the environment at the time of year or of the festival. Dyed muslins or silk veils are loosely arranged as the background and tablecloth. The colours in the summer would be a sunny yellow sky and a light green cloth for the earth. In winter, it would be a snowy white and pale blue sky. At Christmas there would be a deep blue sky with stars, and green and brown cloths on the table. At Diwali the colours would be red and gold and so on.

The four elements are also usually included in some way: earth (stones and crystals), water (could be a bowl or a blue silk cloth), fire (a candle for lighting at special times) and air (a mobile which also tends to change seasonally), and humans or animals (people, gnomes, fairies, ducks and other animals). The children do not play with the scene, as it is created specially by the teacher, but are encouraged to look out for special seasonal 'gifts' to be brought, shells, crystals, pine cones, conkers, apples and berries, and always fresh seasonal flowers.

The outside environment

The outside environment should be as 'natural' as possible. Facilities will include a sandpit, a digging area, trees to climb, a fire pit, a compost area, fruit trees and an organic vegetable garden. Flowers are grown throughout the year for bringing inside for the seasonal and eating table. Occasionally you will find purpose built climbing equipment and swings if space allows. There is usually a hut of some kind where the children can escape to when raining or to play in as a Wendy house. The children, if fortunate enough, build with teacher or parent a willow hut or tunnel, and occasionally you will find a bread oven where bread can be cooked and eaten outside.

The parents often join the teachers and children at work in the garden, and this helps to create a good community spirit.

Chapter 6

Rhythm, repetition and reverence (the three Rs of Steiner Waldorf early childhood)

These key themes underpin the education and are an important educational principle. It gives structure and form to children's daily life and enables them to feel secure and safe, and to know where they are in the world. Children need the reassurance of continuity and regular events mark the kindergarten day, week and year.

Rhythm

In the *Oxford English Dictionary*, rhythm is defined as follows:

- a measured flow of words or phrases in verse or prose determined by various relations of long or short or accented and unaccented syllables

- musically – accented or duration of notes

- physiologically – movement with a regular succession of strong or weak elements (heart/pulse)

- a regularly recurring sequence of events

- art: a harmonious correlation of parts.

Rhythm is the regular recurrence of an event which goes through a cycle within a space of time. There are many different rhythms which dominate our lives:

- the daily rhythm of day and night (and within it of eating, getting up and going to sleep, and the small rhythms within this, such as brushing teeth and washing hands)

■ the rhythm of the seasons going through a cycle within the year

■ festivals and celebrations which occur regularly throughout our lives, such as birthdays and the religious and cultural festivals such as Christmas and Diwali

■ rhythms which also mediate between polar activities, birth and death, rest and movement and so on. They clearly have a quality of orderliness.

In the body, we are also governed by rhythm, predominantly the rhythm of the heart (heartbeat) and the breathing rhythm of inhalation and exhalation, which occurs for the most part unconsciously. There is also the rhythm of the menstrual cycle. These rhythms govern our lives.

Before birth

Rhythm begins before birth, for there is rhythm already in the womb – this is the mother's rhythm, which governs the embryo, and later the foetal rhythm of sound: the heart, blood pumping, both of the foetus and of the mother.

After birth

After birth we have to establish our own rhythm but the baby needs help from the mother – otherwise the mother (and the baby) will be driven to distraction from not knowing what will happen when. This begins the establishment of regular habits such as feeding, sleep, activity etc.

Toddlers

For toddlers, rhythms are established in the daily activities and in the routine of the week such as washing day, shopping day, parent and toddler group day, baking day, cleaning day. They become aware of the rhythm of singing, rhyming, swinging, washing, sweeping, polishing etc., and they are settled and reassured by the routines still supported by the care-taker (parent, childminder and others). They become more consciously aware of the changing seasons, of celebrations and festivals, of daily events, and they are reassured by this for it begins to give a structure to their lives.

The daily rhythm in the kindergarten

There is a varied pace to the rhythmical structure of the day, periods of contraction and expansion which provide a balance between times of activity and times of rest. This might mean that creative play would be followed by a painting activity, or energetic outdoor play by a quiet puppet show. There is a rhythmic alternation between the 'child's time' (creative play, outside time) and the teacher's time (ring time, story), the teacher's time being comparatively short at this age. Working with rhythm helps children to live with change, to find their place in the world, and to begin to understand the past, present and future. It provides a very real foundation for the understanding of time – what has gone before and what will follow – and helps children to relate to the natural and the human world. Attention to rhythm promotes healthy development and leads to a balanced life later. Rhythm helps to harmonise the early will forces (which drive young children into constant activity) and to stabilise their feeling life.

Rhythm in the kindergarten is a swinging activity between contraction and expansion; we need both to become balanced. If there is too much breathing in (contraction), we have a tendency to become quiet, retiring, inward, anti-social, anxious and physically cold. However, if there is too much breathing out (expansion) we can become sociable, relaxed and warm, or in the extreme overstimulated and hyperactive. However, all natural breathing is done unconsciously in a relaxed way, and this is also the case in the kindergarten, where the child is unaware of the rhythmic structure in place but settles happily into it.

So rhythm is used within the day to aid this healthy development of the child's rhythmic system and also as a tool to make life easier for teachers and parents. There is a structure to the day which allows little space for chaos (although we are not absolutely static or rigid in this!) – if the teacher is unprepared, and there are gaps in the rhythmic flow of the day, we really feel it! It allows space for anything to happen!

Space and time mean little to young children; for instance, when they ask what time it is, they do not want to know literally, but want to know if it is time for tea (because they are hungry) or for bed (because they are sleepy, although they will usually deny this while yawning continually). They are the centre of their universe, and whatever happens around them needs to relate directly to their needs.

The teacher is the centre of the kindergarten and therefore must be well prepared to build up the rhythm creatively; at home rhythm is the perfect aid to easier parenting. If the child *always* goes to bed at 7 pm, then he or she will start yawning at that time and will usually go to bed without a fuss (until he or she is ten years old if you are lucky! At exactly 8.30 pm my daughter regularly used to say 'I'm not tired' while yawning profusely).

The child's rhythms are already broken by the staggered kindergarten sessions, and the break at weekends, so what is offered is the rhythm of the morning, the rhythm of the week (baking etc.) the rhythm of the seasons and the rhythm of the year, which provides stability in an ever-changing social and family life.

The child becomes confident, strong and secure, moving freely and orientating easily within the form and structure of the kindergarten. The world becomes familiar and the child feels safe.

Repetition

In the *Oxford English Dictionary*, repetition is defined as follows:

- the act or instance of repeating or being repeated. The thing repeated
- a piece to be learned by heart
- the ability of a musical instrument or voice to repeat a note. To say something out loud, to do something again, to say aloud something heard
- to aid memory or repeat without thinking (repeat parrot fashion).

Repetition plays a key role in establishing continuity and in the healthy development of memory. Children's memories are strengthened by recurring experiences; and daily, weekly and yearly events in kindergarten are remembered and often eagerly anticipated a second time around. Stories are told not just once, but many times; repetition brings the opportunity for children to familiarise themselves with the material and to deepen their relationship to it.

Repetition is a general aid to learning and memory and when we repeat something often enough, it becomes a habit. Repetition strengthens and educates the will forces of the child; it takes will to repeat tasks. Repetition occurs not only daily (the daily routine), but also weekly in the daily activities (e.g. Monday – baking; Tuesday – painting, Wednesday – crafts, Thursday – cooking, Friday – gardening and cleaning) which are repeated on the same days throughout the year, and yearly in the repeated seasonal activities, festivals and celebrations. This again gives the children security and stability within the familiar.

How rhythm and repetition (contraction and expansion) work within the kindergarten day

The kindergarten staff often meet in the morning to say a verse together, to prepare materials and to bring the right mood into the room before the children's arrival. The children are brought into the kindergarten by their parent or carer. They leave the outside behind by taking off shoes and hanging up coats before being brought into the room and handed over to the care of the teacher, who greets each child in turn. (There is always a moment for a quick word between parent and teacher if required.) Many children do not have the rhythmical walk to school anymore, and usually come in somewhat stressed from being 'hurried' to school (how often do parents catch themselves saying 'hurry up, we will be late!'?). The children are drawn to join the activity of the teacher and assistant, who are usually involved in the daily preparation of the snack or activity at this time. Cooking, drawing, sewing, woodwork or weaving are possibilities until they have relaxed enough to join or begin the play.

The **creative play** can be seen as an expansion, a breathing out within the kindergarten room. The children now have freedom (within the structure) to develop their own play constructively. The teachers interfere as little as possible but are there to guide the play if necessary. As mentioned in Chapter 3, the role of teachers is a different one here, for they are doing adult work such as sewing, mending or helping where required; they interrupt play only to guide the children through various social situations if necessary. (They also use this time to observe the children carefully, which is recorded later.) During this time the children re-enact what they have observed in the outside world, learning negotiating skills, caring and sharing, establishing societies and social interaction, which are all aids to future good citizenship. (The kindergarten is a community where each member has an important contribution to make.)

The **daily activity** is introduced during this time, and for some of these the children come together to the tables as a group. These activities could be baking, a seasonal craft or painting and drawing, creating a particularly peaceful creative mood. The children sit at the table and the activities are introduced with suitable songs and finger rhymes. The activities help the children to gain control and mobility of their fingers and learn new skills.

Before continuing with the day, the play materials and activities need to be tidied away, and in many kindergartens the children and teacher come together and refuel a little by eating a few raisins or sunflower seeds (always a good opportunity for counting) and in some cases have a chat to the tidy gnome puppet. This calling to the circle happens through singing: the teacher sings using a lullaby tune 'everybody come to the circle ... everybody come and sit by me' and repeats this until all the children have gathered quietly on the carpet. The children do this in a dreamy way, and hardly ever react with 'I'm not finished playing yet!'. Repetition of the same song, and the daily rhythm help. After the mini-snack, finger game or gentle conversation, either with the puppet or directly with the teacher and their friends, the children, imitating the teacher and assistant, begin to tidy the playthings away, again with a song.

> **I met a little dusty gnome, he said it's time to clean our room,**
> **Round, round, round, whish, whish, whish, clean our room.**

> (Schreiner: 'Spindrift', Wynstones Press)

Or

> **Tidy time, it's tidy time, let us tidy up today,**
> **Let us put it all away ... It's tidy time**

> (Nicol)

The teachers and children **tidy up** properly, putting each item into its correct basket, container, house or shop. This becomes an activity, not a chore, and caring for the environment is an important consideration. Sorting and counting, folding and rolling cloths, matching items and dressing dolls, are all important to get the room ready for play the next day.

During the tidy time the children also set the table for the snack. It is usually the older children who are given this task; often if a younger child wishes to help he or she does so out of imitation of the older children. Here is another opportunity for counting, laying the table with the right number of cups and plates, chairs and spoons. The table is always beautifully decorated with flowers, a candle, and sometimes even a display of animals, little figures, or seasonal objects in the centre.

Ring time comes next. This contains both rhythm and repetition. Now is the opportunity for expansion and contraction within the circle, with the teacher as the focus. Gesture, movement and speech must be clear, precise, beautiful and meaningful – worthy of imitation. In the ring time, which is repeated over two or even three weeks, the children have the opportunity to learn other languages and trace the seasons or act out the stories which have been told. The children learn through the repetition and this aids their memory. It is within ring time that many of the pre-literacy skills which will be needed for later, more formal literacy are developed, such as listening, rhyme, letter sounds, alphabet, counting, rhythms in music (pulse and beat) and interacting with each other in the circle games played. The ring time is usually seasonal and by repeating them the children 'absorb' an enormous store of the rhymes and songs which are contained in it. There is movement which helps the physical development and large and small motor skills are used – from finger games to balancing, jumping, hopping and skipping as well as being aware of each other in space. The ring time begins and ends with a verse to greet each other and the new day:

Good morning dear Earth and good morning dear Sun
Good morning dear stones and flowers everyone
Good morning dear animals, and birds on the tree
Good morning to you and good morning to me.

('Gateways', Wynstones Press)

And it can end:

Two little hands, as dirty as can be,
That's because they have been [baking/drawing/painting
etc.] you see,
So we must wash them, and make a wee.

(Nicol)

From the ring time, a long line of children lead to the toilet, singing all the time. Getting the children to go to the toilet or wash hands is never a problem; it is a rhythm ingrained through constant repetition. We simply can't eat until our hands are clean! As there is no questioning them as to whether they need to go or not, there is no argument.

The children come together again for **snack time**. This is an opportunity for social interaction, to nourish the physical body, to listen and be heard. The serviettes are given out, often by an older child – matching name to child. The meal starts with a blessing on the food, lighting a candle as a focus for thanksgiving, and saying thank you for the meal together when it is finished. (Even the youngest children will sit at the table for over half an hour without fidgeting – they all do it!)

> Blessings on the blossom and blessings on the fruit,
> And blessings on the leaf and stem, and blessings on the root
> And blessings on our meal.

(Patterson: 'Spindrift', Wynstones Press)

The children's physical development is nourished and supported through the largely organic food which they receive in the kindergarten. The new or younger children are fussy at first, but soon eat even the crustiest bread, salad from the garden, apple skins, muesli and vegetable soup! (for they see the other children doing it and imitation is a powerful stimulus!) and nothing is wasted. What is left goes out for the birds or compost. When everyone has finished, the group once again holds hands and says 'thank you' for the meal. The candle is snuffed out and the children take their cups and plates to the kitchen area. Once again, some older children remain for a while to help with the cleaning as the others get ready to go outside.

Garden time comes next, and everyone goes outside. It is important that the children are able to experience all the extremes of the weather, and they are expected to be properly dressed in waterproof clothing, hats and gloves in the winter, and sunhats and sleeves in the summer. This is a perfect opportunity for them to learn to tie laces, do up zips and buttons and when they have managed it themselves, to help the younger children. Quite a lot of time is allowed for this. Wellington boots are worn most of the time as the play tends to get rather muddy, and they do a great deal of digging! Now the children are expected to be *doing*, actively experiencing their physical bodies and the space around them. Young children do not have a good awareness of space (noticeable by the way they often bump into things or each other, or trip over steps or objects) so the teachers and children work on this by throwing balls, playing ring games, skipping with ropes (big and small), balancing, climbing, gardening and strengthening the limbs. These all help the children to become confident in their bodies and develop new skills. Sometimes the children are taken on walks to the park, and they learn road awareness and listening skills too. In most kindergartens the children tend an organic vegetable garden. They dig the ground over, plant the seeds, water, weed, and eventually harvest the fruit and vegetables for eating. Digging up potatoes is a favourite. Finding worms to break up the soil, hunting ladybirds and caterpillars, feeding the birds and hedgehogs, and caring for the pond so that they can watch the frogs and toads spawn and the tadpoles grow gives much joy. There is always a sandpit, a gravel or mud pit for 'digging to Australia' and trees to climb (with the appropriate risk assessments, of course). The children have access to large planks and sticks for building tents and tepees, rocks and bricks for walls, spades, forks and rakes for digging, and water. The teacher and assistant work alongside the children in the garden, always occupied, and observing everything.

The children return to the kindergarten room for **story time**. After washing hands and changing into indoor clothes, they gather together in a ring, sit quietly and listen to a story told (not read) by the teacher. This is an opportunity for the children to completely 'switch off' physically and enter a dream world of fantasy and imagination where they can build pictures inwardly. Here stories learned by heart are told to the children, or puppet shows are performed, repeating them sometimes for a week or more until they become a friend and a companion. Stories are chosen carefully (folk, nature or fairy tales) and the vocabulary is vast. The fairy tales carry deep moral truths within them and set before the children a picture of how the person can develop himself or herself to do a task worthy of humankind. Puppet shows, sometimes the showing of beautiful books with moving pictures, and plays enhance the children's understanding of stories. Children whose first language is not English are given extra help where necessary by giving a copy of the story, and sometimes a translation, to the parent to read to the child at home, and the repeated nature of the storytelling supports their acquisition of English.

After the story has finished, we sing a goodbye song:

> Goodbye to you, goodbye to you, we'll see you soon
>   again
> It's time to go so don't be late, we'll wave goodbye at the
>   garden gate
> Goodbye to you, goodbye to you, we'll see you soon
>   again.

(Nicol)

A quiet game is often played until all those going home have been collected. The children who remain for afternoon care make up a little bed with mattress, blanket and pillow, and lie down for a rest before the afternoon session. The parents are encouraged to continue the rhythm at home, and are reminded that the children have been working hard at play all morning, for this is children's 'work', and the afternoon needs to be peaceful with lots of outside play, or going for a walk, for walking has its own rhythm. Hyperactivity can be a result of lack of activity, and walking is a rhythmic healthy activity. The parents are encouraged not to fill the afternoons with further activities as the children need to absorb the experiences of the morning without further stimulation.

Another way in which rhythm and repetition is brought into the day is through singing. Singing is a subtle way of penetrating the consciousness of children without awakening them too much. It is gentle and repetitive and the songs used are very, very simple. Calling songs tend to be in the tune of the minor third and fifth chords. If you called 'coo-ee' to your neighbour across the garden, you usually do this in the dropped minor third (top D down to B or top D down to B and G (5th) on the piano).

Singing contains both rhythm and repetition. When you sing, you cannot really be angry or upset. We use singing in the kindergarten to 'break through' situations, call children to attention, calm things down, communicate and give instructions . . . and we sing with joy! Our feeling life (emotion) is involved with the rhythmic system. Music is emotionally involving – often when we listen to music, our breathing imitates it. Singing used in the right way can be calming. However, we don't sing all the time; then it just becomes background noise, and the children 'switch it off'.

Reverence

Reverence for the child

Rudolf Steiner asked teachers to 'receive each child with reverence' and look not only at the physical body of the child, but also at the spirit and soul. These qualities all make up the human being, and all need nurturing. He asked teachers to see the child coming towards them from a spiritual world, and this image is uniquely portrayed in an extract from 'Ode – Intonations of Immortality' from *Songs of Innocence and Experience* by William Wordsworth:

> Our birth is but a sleep and a forgetting;
> The soul that rises with us, our life's star
> Hath had elsewhere its setting
> And cometh from afar;
> Not in entire forgetfulness,
> And not in utter nakedness
> But trailing clouds of glory do we come
> From God who is our home:
> Heaven lies about us in our infancy!

In many kindergartens, as an integral part of the room, will be a framed print of Raphael's *Sistine Madonna*. This is another representation of a picture of the child, surrounded by angels and held with love in the arms of his mother. Children are comforted by this unconsciously, and the teachers use it as a form of meditative study. 'Where has the child come from, where is he going, and what can I do to support this?'

The picture of the child as a threefold being enables teachers to see each as more than the physical body standing before them, as bearing a bag of gifts which the teacher can help him or her to unwrap; enhancing and developing those gifts is our task with each child. This was once described to me by Estelle Bryer, who wrote a letter to her nine-year-old granddaughter, who was concerned that she was not doing well at a school subject.

> Every person is born with a bag of gifts. Some never even open their bags, and their unused gifts vanish. Others work hard at opening their gifts and using them wisely, and when one is worked with properly, another always appears. Other gifts are only ready to be found in later life. The most important thing is to have a golden heart . . . that is given to many as a gift but we have to work hard at polishing it with good deeds so that it can always shine . . . it makes our eyes sparkle!

In the kindergarten day there are moments of reverence, and the teachers lovingly create opportunities for the children to experience joy, awe and wonder. Wonder is a reverential experience, and enabling the children to experience life itself in all its beauty, to create that 'ahhh' moment at any opportunity, brings a sense of peace and joy to the child's learning about life's eternal possibilities.

These reverential moments are also awakened during celebrations and festivals, both cultural and religious, and the celebration of the child's birthday is one occasion that both the parent and child will remember for ever.

The child's birthday in a kindergarten

Celebrations are performed a little differently by each teacher. I will describe one way of doing it.

Before the child comes into the classroom on either the morning of the birthday or soon afterwards (never before), the teacher has prepared a birthday table, decorated and with a special cloth, flowers, a birthday candle, a birthday crown. Space has been left for the cake brought from home, and a card with a drawing for the child (done by the teacher) and with a birthday poem that in some way draws on the child's gifts, and a small present made by the teacher. In my kindergarten we had different gifts for each age. A finger-puppet bird for those turning four, a bean bag with ribbons (for throwing) for those turning five and always something special for the six-year-olds such as a special wooden whistle, a boat or a handmade figure for playing with. Prior to the day, the parent has provided the teacher with a 'potted history' of special events marking the child's development.

The parent has the opportunity to spend the morning and accompanies the child to kindergarten. During the first part of the morning, the children draw a card for the birthday child, or a birthday book is made from drawings by all the children. This is placed on the birthday table as well, and when it is ring time, children and teacher form a ring, say the verse as normal, and then hold hands singing a special song for the child:

> Today is a happy, happy, happy day . . . today is a happy
>   day,
> And why is it a happy, happy, happy day . . . and why is it
>   a happy day?
> Because it's Debbie's happy birthday, it's Debbie's happy
>   birthday.

The parent then sits in the centre of the ring of children, while the birthday child and their chosen best friend (their angel) go to the outside of the ring. The angel is given wings and a star crown to wear. The teacher ceremoniously lights the birthday candle and gives it to the parent. Then the birthday child, led by the angel, weaves in and out of the children standing in the circle, while they sing this song:

> In heaven shines a golden star, an angel brought me from
>   afar
> From heaven high unto the earth, and brought me to my
>   house of birth.

> (Patterson: 'Gateways', Wynstones Press)

The angel brings the child to the parent who hands the child the 'light of life' and they carefully carry the candle to the birthday table (this is a moment of such joy and wonder that most parents are quite overcome with emotion). Then it is time to put on the birthday crown and look at the presents and cards. The birthday candle is put in a safe place until the meal.

During snack time, once all the children are sitting and all is quiet, the birthday candle is brought to the table and the children hear the developmental story. This begins with the little angel journeying from heaven, having collected gifts for her future life on earth from the sun, moon and stars. She crosses the rainbow bridge and is born into the arms of her new family. Thereafter follows the milestones and rather fun achievements which the parent has given to the teacher, and is woven into a story of the child to date. With each birthday, a candle is lit on the cake, and when all are lit, the traditional happy birthday song is sung, and the candles are blown out. At the end of the day, the child takes everything home.

Reverence for each other

In facilitating the personal, social and moral development of the children, the teachers endeavour to be a role model worthy of imitation, and make sure that their relationships with the parents, children and their colleagues are respectful, caring, empathetic and warm. The children hopefully imitate this and through their creative play and daily social activities learn to interact positively with each other. In kindergarten they are encouraged to share, to work together and to co-operate with each other, also establishing effective relationships with their teachers and other adults.

The older children who are already familiar with kindergarten increasingly assume the role of helpers. They look after the younger children, which is particularly important for children who grow up without older brothers and sisters. Working with the social will forces of the six-year-olds by encouraging the attitude of caring, listening to and helping others, provides the child with a basis for more conscious empathy and social awareness in later years, and if practised enough it develops into unconscious good habits.

Reverence for the environment

The environment and environmental issues are important for the well-being and the future of our earth, and in the kindergarten emphasis is placed on caring for the physical surroundings inside and outside. The kindergarten needs to be cared for, as do its contents. The toys are fixed, and being mostly wood are easily polished and mended, unlike plastic toys, which generally have to be thrown away when broken. Buttons and torn clothing are sewn and washed (doll's, children's and fabrics used by the children), and the kindergarten is cleaned as a weekly activity (polished, swept daily and the floors, walls equipment and windows washed) all with the children. The garden is cared for, the birds fed with breadcrumbs, the compost tended and everything recycled, which introduces children to the idea of ecology and forms an important part of the curriculum. Nothing is wasted.

Reverence for the food

Nature is thanked for providing the children with good food to eat (see verse above). It is grown in the garden and tended with care. It is harvested, cooked and enjoyed by all. The children sit and eat in a social way at the table until all have finished. The older children take turns in serving the bread or fruit, taking it round to the others at the table, and pouring their drinks. 'Thank you' is commonly heard.

Chapter 7

Celebration of festivals

Festivals and celebrations mark the passing of time. They are fondly remembered throughout our lives as significant 'happenings', be they seasonal, cultural or celebrations such as birthdays and christenings, bar mitzvahs, anniversaries or even funerals.

Celebrating festivals with children helps to establish continuity, a rhythm and repetition, which give form and structure to their lives. These two, as well as reverence, are significantly present in all festivals and celebrations.

To celebrate a festival with children we have to be active in it, as children learn by being active in their will, their doing. Festivals need to be a complete artistic experience, to appeal to all the senses and we need to consider all the things which make up a festival:

■ history

■ food

■ costumes

■ music

■ mood (colour)

■ story/puppet play.

Religious, cultural and seasonal festivals

In the spring and summer, there are fewer festivals than in the autumn and winter. The summer festivals are significant in their outwardness – reaching out to humanity in a gesture of sacrifice and rebirth (spring/Easter), brotherhood and community (Whitsun) and St John's (mid-summer) reaching out to each other in a gesture of empathy. Harvest and Michaelmas lead towards Martinmas (the lantern festival where St Martin shared his light, food and clothing with the poor), and Advent in the winter, looking inward at the little spark of light to which gives birth at Christmas with the coming of Jesus bringing love as a gift to the earth. Candlemas and the spring festivals lead once again to new life and resurrection. These are the most common festivals celebrated in a Steiner kindergarten.

Multicultural festivals should be an integral part of the kindergarten where a child is welcomed from another faith or culture. It is important to involve the parents and families through acknowledging, understanding and accepting their festivals (religious, seasonal and social) and then living into them so that they can become a reality for all concerned.

There are many similarities between festivals of different cultures, and often the themes overlap. Diwali, Martinmas, Channuka and Advent occur at the same time of the year, bringing light into the darkness.

The development of a festival

As mentioned above, thought, care and careful preparation go into the development and implementation of a festival when undertaken with the children. Below I have written a description of one of the festivals which I developed for my own kindergarten.

The festival of Diwali

Three children in the kindergarten celebrated the festival of Diwali in some form at home. My first thought was how to begin to relate to this festival when I had little knowledge of the culture, history and so on, so I enlisted the help of the parents in developing my own understanding, and also undertook some research.

History

Diwali or Deepavali falls sometime between October and November on a moonless night. (Nature makes it the darkest night but humankind makes it the brightest!) Diwali means 'Row of Light' or ' Festival of Light' and is widely celebrated by Hindus throughout the world (and by almost everyone, so I'm told, in India). It contains age-old symbols: the triumph of light over darkness and of good over evil. The story of Rama and Sita is told and the goddess Lakshmi worshipped. Homes are cleaned and decorated, lamps and lights are acquired and food is prepared. There are celebrations with feasts, lights, dancing and fireworks.

Many of the above fit well into the kindergarten at this time of year as we prepare for Martinmas, Guy Fawkes and Advent; however, we found the story of Rama and Sita too complicated for our kindergarten children, so I wrote my own, which was told leading up to and on the day of the festival.

The story

Once upon a time there lived a mother and father who had many children, and the youngest was called Anju. One day Anju woke to find that everyone was busy, cleaning and dusting, painting and scrubbing, sewing and cooking. 'Ma, what is happening?' he asked. 'Anju, tonight I will tell you.' said mother, and so she did.

That night when Anju was tucked up in bed, his mother told him the story of the festival of Diwali.

'Anju, we need to clean our house to be ready for a visit from Lakshmi, for she will bring us wealth and plenty, nice clothes, food to eat and happiness to our family. But she will only visit houses that are clean and tidy. Lazy people who never work and don't bother to clean and tidy their homes never have a visit from Lakshmi, and so are never happy and they always grumble about how they live. If we are kind and cheerful, however, she will shower blessings over us.'

'How can she see how clean our house is, Ma?' asked Anju. 'At Diwali we light our houses with lamps filled with oil, or many candles, so that every corner is bright, that is why we make lots of little clay dishes to hold the candles or oil in. Tomorrow you will see. Goodnight Anju,' said his mother.

The next day Anju woke early and the house was already filled with joyous sounds. He put on his new clothes and helped to draw the rangoli designs with coloured sand on the floor. And when they had laid out the food and flowers everywhere, they put the oil lamps and candles onto every shelf and into every corner so that the house was filled with rows and rows of lights. In the evening Mother and Father lit them all and soon the friends began to arrive bringing gifts of sweet things for the family. Anju handed round food and more sweets to the visitors and they all made music together and danced and talked until quite late.

Anju was tired when everyone went outside, 'It's so dark, Ma,' he said. 'Not for long, Anju,' said his mother.

And suddenly the sky was filled with bangs and whizzes as fireworks lit up the dark sky, raining stars down on the children below. Anju and his brothers and sisters took sparklers to the children who had none, so that they could light up the darkness too, and those children's smiles lit up Anju's heart.

That night, when his mother tucked Anju up in bed he asked sleepily; 'Ma, did Lakshmi come to our house? I didn't see her.' And his mother answered 'Of course she did Anju, for when happiness, light and love enter our hearts it is Lakshmi who puts it there. Didn't you feel it today?' But there was no reply, for Anju was fast asleep.

Preparation

In the kindergarten we made clay Divas (the lamps to hold nightlights) and cleaned the kindergarten – even the cobwebs in the corners! The nature table was covered with drapes of red and gold, and the parents supplied me with material and donated costumes and instruments.

The day of the festival

On the morning the children arrived to a very decorated room, red muslins and lots of gold and brass, the clothes laid out and flowers and lamps everywhere. We set the table and prepared the food, buttered the warm naan bread (different flavours) and cut up exotic fruit. We then washed and dressed in our bright Indian clothes – muslins and scarves, saris and hats, draped with care. Then we lit the main candle and to the recorder and bells we danced together, holding and waving our brightly coloured sashes to Indian songs we had learned. Weaving in and out of a circle, we made star patterns (joined by some of our parents who really knew what they were doing!). Then each child lit his or her light from the big candle and carried it to the table, and soon it was lit with a long row of candles. We ate warmed naan bread and fruit and it was all delicious.

At story time, when the children returned from outside, they found the room in darkness, and in the centre of the story ring was a ring of their lit candles, and in the centre of that was a big pot with sticks in it!

After the story we lit those sticks . . . sparklers! (indoor of course) And when we came to blow out the candles to take home – oh, what a surprise, jellied fruits, one for each child.

Lakshmi had visited our kindergarten this day.

Chapter 8
Storytelling and puppetry

Storytelling

Storytelling is and always has been a central activity of human life – it is one of the ways in which we learn about the world and make sense of our experiences. By giving children the experience of listening we enliven their imaginations and fantasy and educate their memory – we help them to understand their world and to become effective communicators and listeners.

Family or stories from personal experience are the easiest way to begin, and children love nothing more than to hear about themselves. It is easy to develop these stories and to add to them, thus bringing in some fantasy. This is a good way to bring in an event which is about to happen (holiday, hospital), to moralise a little (brush teeth, accident crossing the road) or to encourage positive behaviour (putting on the clothes laid out, being kind to friends etc.).

Next is learning stories, so that they can be told rather than read to the children. The reason for this is that it enables the children to form their own pictures. There is nothing wrong with reading stories to the child either, but the effort of learning the story beforehand engages the will and allows you to add something of yourself to the story, which is felt inwardly by the child. Reading together and showing the child the pictures (we call it 'reading the pictures') shows the children how to care for and handle books properly.

Animal stories (not fables, which come at a later age) are always fun, for animals appeal to the feeling nature of the child, they can get up to mischief, be naughty and get away with it – something we 'moral' humans can't. Folk tales bring alive other cultures and broaden their world.

Fairy tales are told to older children and helps their inner life to become flexible and active. This gives wings to feeling, fires the will, stimulates the thinking, and allows them to experience emotions such as joy, sympathy, fear and courage, which works on their inner life allowing them to develop a moral discernment of good and evil and an inner strength, a courage to overcome and face the tasks and tests of life to come.

The stories we choose in the kindergarten are not moralising or cautionary tales, but bearers of underlying moral truths. These truths are not explained but are left to continue working in the child's imagination, their feeling and will. Dr Von Kugelgen, from the International Waldorf Kindergarten Association, quoted Steiner as saying:

> Fairytales are healing to the soul of a child … The human soul has an in-extinguishable need to have the substance of fairy tales flow through its veins, just as the body needs to have nourishing substances circulate through it.

> (Von Kugelgen 1993: 47)

The fairy tale engenders a dreamlike, experiential consciousness, which radiates feeling, and is filled with images.

The wisdom in fairy tales speaks figuratively of change, of enchantment, and solution – and with this, the secret of humanity. The child can sympathise with it right away; all the 'cruelty' which we see in the dance around the wolf at the end of Red Riding Hood is for the child nothing other than the victory of good over bad:

> 'Fairy-tale children' experience more, they can express themselves more fully either in words or through art, are open, can listen better, and display greater pleasure in creative endeavours. They form thoughts into well-structured sentences containing a more extensive vocabulary.

> (Von Kugelgen 1993: 48)

When telling fairy tales, it is important not to arouse fear by using drama in the voice. They are told with a gentle dreamy lilting 'storytelling voice'.

There are certain fairy tales suitable for different ages. The teacher needs to choose stories that work with the children and which suit their age or individual characteristics. The most important consideration is the storyteller's own relationship to the story. The teacher needs to understand it and be comfortable with it.

Puppetry

For centuries now, puppet plays have been a source of pleasure. It does not matter whether the text is in one language or another, whether the story is presented in a shopping centre or in a palace, or whether the puppets are worked by strings, worn on the hands, moved by rods or whatever; puppets are always fascinating to human beings. For these miniature actors are surrounded by an atmosphere of reality and fantasy, of magic, mystery and dreams and, in addition, the humour and satire afford delightful entertainment.

In these little figures there is a mysterious power, which can cast such a spell over children and grown-ups alike that they are bewitched into imagining living creatures of flesh and blood in place of puppets made of wood or other materials. The audience see only what they want to see; indeed they are so gripped by the play that the imagination makes its own contribution and they see much more: they see laughing and weeping and the whole gamut of emotions mirrored in the puppet faces.

In recent years there has been a gratifying increase in the number of amateur puppet groups; these groups are a living source of creative and artistic talent and their number is growing from day to day. One finds puppet groups in children's hospitals, in the treatment for disturbances, special needs, traffic education, war torn countries, Aids education, therapy for speech defects and much more, where a child can put a hand into a puppet and take on a different role, to talk and act as he or she wishes and 'it's all safe'. When a child 'talks to' a puppet, the puppet actually acts as a mediator, as a third person. The child therefore does not feel confronted by another ego, but feels free to speak or react safely, and will not be judged.

In an article (on the art of the Marionette theatre, Von Kugelgen (1993) quoted Steiner as saying, 'Puppetry is a remedy against the ravages of civilisation'. Steiner always responded to questions which were asked of him; in 1917, Leonhard Gem and Hedwig Hauck (painters and sculptors) asked Steiner for advice on how to build a puppet theatre for a day care centre (actually the children were from 4 to 12 years old). Steiner got deeply involved in this, and insisted that the marionettes must hang from threads tied directly to the fingers (not a crossbar), directed from above, that only marionettes were appropriate for the presentation of fairy tales, and that a narrator should read the story from outside the curtain.

Steiner was particularly interested in stage lighting and scenery, and everything was done with one purpose in mind; he said, 'we must do everything in our power to help the children to develop fantasy!'.

Puppet shows nourish the feeling life and the senses. They contain music, colour and movement – a full artistic experience. The movement of the puppets should be peaceful (not jerky like cartoons or fast like Punch and Judy). The children take these movements into their beings, and it affects their own sense of movement. Puppetry helps develop the memory and increases vocabulary and communication skills.

In the kindergarten many different forms of puppetry are used: finger and hand puppets, tabletop puppet shows and full fairy tales done with marionettes. In play little figures are used to make up scenes on the floor and they interact with each other. This is particularly suitable for the younger children.

However presented, puppet shows are a full artistic experience. The scene is made (sometimes with the children) and then covered with a cloth – the 'unveiling' when it begins, usually to music played simply on a lyre (children's harp) or kalimba (a type of thumb piano), draws the children into the puppet show. It has a beginning, middle and end, which is complete and satisfying for them, containing language, movement, music and colour; the teacher or adult is responsible for what happens, which gives the children a feeling of security. The children can see how adults deal with mistakes, which reassures them that things are not always perfect; everything is visible to them. They get a picture of the whole, and the past, present and future is before them.

Very often the larger puppet shows are presented after the story has been told a few days before. The repetition of the story helps the memory and enables the children to build their own pictures before they are presented with visual ones. Because of the repetition they can re-create the stories in play or their own puppet shows. They do not use the teachers' puppets but adapt or make their own.

The puppet pocket apron (worn by the adult) has decorated pockets in which the finger or standing puppets 'live'. They come out to tell stories or sing rhymes. A familiar story can also be told using the puppets in different pockets to tell the story. There are farm aprons, tree aprons, house aprons and so on. Silk cloths are used to cover the lap on which to act out the story.

Puppetry is enriching not only for the children but also for the puppeteers, for there is no end to the creativity.

Chapter 9

Working within the Foundation Stage curriculum and towards the early learning goals

Since the introduction of the voucher scheme with its desirable learning outcomes, and then the Foundation Stage Curriculum, some Steiner Waldorf kindergartens have begun registering for the early years funding for three- and four-year-olds. The Steiner Waldorf Schools Fellowship was and continues to be involved in the consultations with the curriculum guidance, Foundation Stage, *Birth to Three Matters*, the DfES and Ofsted Inspectors.

There is little difficulty in meeting some and working towards all the learning goals, with obvious exceptions in areas where there are fundamental curriculum differences. These are the early introduction of IT and electronic gadgetry (we have what we call 'warm' technology, such as woodwork tools, spinning wheels, cookers, juicers etc.) and the introduction of written letters and numbers in a formal way. The following sectors highlight how learning goals are reached with little difficulty and in the most cases with outstanding results in the Ofsted inspection reports.

Personal, social and emotional development

These areas are particularly strong, both in social development, and in the dispositions and attitudes of the children. As you can see in the previous

---

Some of the information in this chapter has been taken from the *Educational Tasks of the Waldorf Curriculum*, by Sally Jenkinson and Martin Rawson (1998).

chapters, the children, working from imitation and supported by staff and peers, are able to become independent learners who form good relationships with adults and peers and thus an integrated and harmonious group. The children have a highly developed moral sense, and are sensitive to the needs and feelings of others. It is wonderful to see the older children in the mixed-age kindergartens helping the younger to dress, with play and developing a general caring attitude.

Communication, language and literacy

Children develop competence in talking, listening and in the ability to use words as they speak freely and learn to listen to others. Good speech and the development of oral skills are promoted; concentration is also on the aural tradition and the children listen to many wonderful stories, which belong to the literary heritage of the culture of childhood.

A well told story creates an appreciation for the human voice and the beauty and rhythms of language. It also helps to extend vocabulary and to aid the development of a good memory. Through storytelling and story hearing, the children partake in the structuring processes of narrative, in which complex information is put into meaningful context. Children leave kindergarten with a rich and varied repertoire of songs, stories and poems; this might also include verses in French or German. These stages of pre-literacy are an important preparation for the formal introduction of reading and writing, which requires clear hearing and speaking, good memory, an intuitive sense for language structure, an enjoyment for language as well as manual skills and hand-eye co-ordination.

Children engage in many activities, such as sewing and weaving, which develop hand–eye co-ordination, manual dexterity and orientation (useful preparation for reading print from left to right). They also discuss their own drawings and take great delight in telling stories by 'reading their pictures'. This activity promotes the development of verbal skills and frees the narrative from the printed text, thus encouraging children to use their own words. Many children also set out or perform puppet shows and develop dramatic skills through working with narrative and dialogue. Painting and drawing help with balance and symmetry and most five-year-olds are able to write their own name. Children experience the musicality of language and its social aspects through playing ring games and doing eurythmy, a form of movement which works with language and music.

The combination of these activities cultivates a love of language, promotes fluency and allows children time to become really familiar with the spoken word – the best preparation and foundation for the subsequent development of literacy. Use of language also affects cognitive development as well chosen words and good syntax support clear thinking.

Mathematical development

Mathematics and the use of mathematical language is integrated into the daily rhythm. It might take place at the table where food is prepared (sliced carrots make wonderful natural circles and have the added virtue of being able to be eaten later in soup!), and addition and subtraction (or more or less), weight, measure, quantity and shape are grasped in a practical manner as part of daily life in cooking and baking. Mealtimes offer an opportunity for the moral, social and mathematical to work together as children engage in place-setting and the sharing of food which has been prepared earlier for everyone to eat.

Through movement games, children recognise and re-create patterns: in, out, alternate, in front of, behind. Natural objects such as acorns, pine cones, conkers and shells are sorted, ordered and counted, as part of spontaneous play. Children are directly involved in mathematical experience and use mathematical language in a natural way which is usually embedded in a social and moral context. Learning experiences for the young child are not separated from the business of daily living; learning gains meaning by its relevance to life.

Knowledge and understanding of the world

Children develop a good relationship to the natural world. They learn to value its gifts and to understand its processes and patterns of change. Domestic tasks provide opportunities for elementary experiences in science and good use is made of the four elements. Family participation is encouraged and teachers, working with parents, create 'birthday stories', which are based on the child's personal biography and are told at special ceremonies to which families are invited. Festivals and community events enable children to begin to know about their own and others' cultures and beliefs. Awe and wonder in the natural world is enhanced through the lack of direct instruction and the use of fantasy and imagination by the adults.

People in the community who practise a particular craft, or who have special skills, are often invited to visit the kindergarten, and many teachers take their children for short local walks and visits. An interest in the natural world, the use of tools and 'warm' technology help the children to find out and explore how their world works.

Physical development

The children have constant opportunities, from domestic tasks and creative experiences, to build up their small and large motor skills, and to practise and enjoy these skills in the physical environment.

Creativity

There are a number of areas where the inspectors have difficulty in understanding or working with the Steiner pedagogy: the use of questioning to enhance and broaden the child's learning, and the lack of display of the children's work. Creating an environment where the children are learning by imitation, where the senses are protected and where there is a sense of peace and lack of clutter, helps this process.

Questioning children

Children learn out of exploration and discovery, and imitation of the adults and the world around them. The Steiner philosophy considers that children do not need adults to question what and why they do things, only to support and encourage, which can be done without words! The environment is already noisy, busy, stimulating; children tend to switch off from these constant stimulations, to build a shell around themselves, to stop listening, to become overstimulated, to constantly expect praise and support – is this what is wanted? No, quiet supportive confirmation of their explorations into life is all that is required. Children just need space, time and the right environment to develop at their own pace.

Why children's work is not displayed

Looking at the pieces of work that children produce one can see not only their skills and developing capacities, but also indications of individual strengths and weaknesses, both currently and in the future. In children's drawings particularly, one can see significant indicators of developmental stages. For these reasons careful note is taken of everything that the children produce which includes paying attention to what the children may want to tell us about their work. It is also part of the reverence and respect that is shown to everyone that children's efforts are appreciated and taken care of, thus setting a good example.

For young children, however, the process is much more important than the result, and viewing the display is less satisfactory than the producing of it. Children often ignore their paintings once completed and shown to an adult. Displays of work also invite comparison and judgements and we believe these should be avoided in children under seven. Instead, after the teacher has appreciated and taken note both of the child at work and of the product of the work, this will either be carefully put ready for the child to take home (pictures may be rolled and tied with wool, other projects wrapped), or the teacher may keep the piece of work to give to the family at the end of term, or the end of the school year, or at the next festival, if the project is directly related to the festival. For example, the pompom chicks may be gathered in a nest of straw as they are completed, ready to give out at the spring festival, or the whole year's spread of paintings (one from each week) will be collected in a folder that the child has made and given to the parents at the end of the school year. Saving the drawings and paintings in this way enables the teacher to gain an overview of the child's progress, which will be discussed at an individual meeting with the parents. Alternatively, children may take their drawings home more frequently, but the teacher will keep those that are particularly developmentally significant in a file as part of a portfolio.

In this way children are shown that their work is valuable and to be taken care of, and that the work of producing it is worthwhile and noted, but they are not encouraged to dwell upon it after it is complete.

Chapter 10

Working with parents

Steiner Waldorf teachers are committed to establishing good relationships with parents and building the bridge between home and school, as the importance of a happy, smooth transition from home to school is recognised. The majority of kindergartens hold baby groups and/or parent and child sessions (birth to three years) and have a good rapport with the family before the child enters kindergarten. Teachers promote and emphasise the importance of close partnerships with parents and provide a focus for parent support. Links are also created with parents through a range of social and school-based events and activities, such as providing parenting or other workshops, craft sessions and celebrating festivals together.

Close liaison between parent and teacher is encouraged and the process of integration into the kindergarten is a gradual one. Teachers inform themselves about the child by meeting with the parents before the child joins the group, and filling out the 'child profile', which includes information on the birth, the developmental steps of the child, the cultural or religious beliefs of the family, medical or environmental influences, behaviour, social skills with their siblings and so on. The child has a slow integration into the group, with the parent visiting with the child if necessary. The teacher and assistant usually do a home visit during the first term, which is an opportunity to develop a closer relationship with the child. Regular parent evenings with a themed talk and activity provides an opportunity for parents to meet on a social basis, as well as familiarising the parents with the curriculum. The parents join the children for some festivals and puppet shows, and help is expected with the upkeep of the kindergarten, such as doing the washing, flower rota, providing organic fruit, joining the group for outings or bringing an activity such as helping with the woodwork or spinning.

Parent and child groups

Most kindergartens begin with, and work closely with, the parent and child group, which is where the children and parents are introduced to the ethos of the pedagogy. This provides a peaceful environment within which parent and child (toddler to around the age of three) can play and talk with each other and to those around them. Because parents are often insecure with their parenting skills, space is offered where parents can find the stillness in which to realise that they are already doing a great job. The leaders offer information and the parents are free to decide what to do with it. Because the impulse of imitation is strong, there is no expectation that the parents compel their child to join in, but rather that they do so themselves. The parents not only sit and chat with each other, but also play with their children. When they are involved in a craft, however, the children either join them out of imitation, or this allows the children the space and freedom to begin more social exploration.

The toys used are simple, as in the kindergarten – carved wooden animals and toys, hand sewn dolls, and natural objects found on walks, e.g. conkers, pine cones and seashells. Lengths of dyed muslin are wrapped around screens to form cosy home corners and little dens.

Making simple crafts helps parents to recognise skills and to bring some of these into their home, such as baking bread, painting and drawing. Nature tables in the home are encouraged, and seasonal crafts which they make, such as the butterflies, mobiles, lanterns and decorations, enhance these. Parent and child sit together, work together and learn together, handling the simplest of natural materials such as brightly coloured sheep's wool, cones and seeds, beeswax, muslin and silk.

In each session there is time for play and craft activity which run alongside each other for nearly 50 minutes. A tidy-up song forms the prelude to circle time. Here the children and parents may listen to the story of a little child and the journey made from home to countryside and back home again, via the animals in the fields and the woods or rivers, mixed with familiar nursery rhymes and seasonal songs of childhood. Properly seated around the table, a snack of freshly baked food is shared, once the blessing has been sung as a reminder of the importance of sharing with one another. The morning finishes with time in the garden, meeting later in the goodbye circle, which is both an affirmation of time together as well as a reminder of future meetings.

It is recognised that parenting is the most important task that each of us can do, and therefore support and guidance is given where necessary or required.

Chapter 11

Assessment and recording the development of the child

All teachers are expected to have an understanding of the development of the healthy child, to observe carefully, to record development in such a way that it is continually living. The children's files contain not only their child profile (taken at the initial interview), but also any comments and meetings with parents, the developmental drawings, the birthday stories, illnesses and milestones, celebrations and events, the first loose tooth, the first haircut and chickenpox; all are given equal importance. The files also detail how the children walk, whether their small and gross motor skills are developing properly, if they have any special needs or disabilities, and the celebration of achievements. Photos are taken, pieces of handwork kept if possible, paintings used as the folder, and all of it shared with the parents.

If the child is not progressing in certain areas, the teachers may introduce an activity which supports this. In its simplest form, the teacher might continue to work with the family, introducing remedial stories or activities, eurythmy or movement, or concentrate on particular speech rhythms or rhymes. However, if there is more reason for concern, the teacher might also recommend that the child is seen by a school doctor, or that further investigation is undertaken. An Individual Education Plan is put in place for this child, and outside agencies brought in to help.

Child study

If a child is experiencing difficulty at any time, the teaching group undertakes a 'child study', the purpose of which is to heighten the awareness of an individual child's needs, physical, emotional, educational or social.

The request for child study time on the agenda of the weekly teachers' meeting is brought either by the child's teacher or by any colleague who recognises the need for a study. It may also be the parents who request it. Two weeks' notice allows everyone to concentrate on the child and observe him or her. The teachers discuss the child with the parents before the meeting, and the purpose and content of the child study is explained – the emphasis is on providing a 'helping hand' rather than an instant solution and care is taken to avoid labelling the child. Parents are encouraged to collaborate by contributing a written (or verbal) report of their own experiences, and of their thoughts, feelings, concerns and hopes for their child. Biographical details about pregnancy, birth and early childhood, health and family circumstances (taken at first interview) are also useful.

Where appropriate, the school doctor will see the child, and parents will be involved in this consultation. A therapist may be assigned to work with the child as part of an overall package of help.

Through sharing individual observations and insights, the teaching group gains a deeper understanding of the child's difficulties. The process of studying as a group, the involvement of the parents and the recommendations resulting from the exercise, together promote better educational practice, increase awareness all round and, crucially, help the child.

Ongoing assessment and the child profile (Foundation Stage)

Most kindergartens complete an ongoing child profile which covers the main areas of development listed in the early learning goals. These are completed in such a way as to reflect the all-round development of the child during his or her years in the kindergarten. At the end of this, the profile is passed on to the next class teacher in a Steiner school, or given to the parent for the child to take to primary school. This allows the next teacher to form a picture of the capabilities and development of the child.

Leaving reports

At the end of their time in the kindergarten, when the children are due to leave, one of the gifts that the child takes from the teacher is the kindergarten 'report'. This usually contains a drawing done by the teacher for the child, a poem or story which is written specially, and will contain a record of the child's achievements and events plus photos to support this.

Transition to 'big' school

During their last year in the kindergarten, the older children often consolidate as a group, particularly if there is more than one kindergarten group attached to a Steiner school. They get together one morning or afternoon each week, to work and play together, and often have more complicated games, have longer stories, make particular projects and so on.

The graduation ceremony, where they leave or go on to the next class, is quite a celebration. Parents and families attend, and children perform a play, a puppet show, songs or a ring time, and receive their poems, cards and gifts. The next class teacher (if children are going into a Steiner school) tells a story reflecting the different journeys children will take into new subjects, ways of learning and social contexts, and then they usually go through a flowered arch, supported by music from the schoolchildren, into the next class. The kindergarten teacher and the other children wave goodbye, and their new teacher greets them.

Chapter 12
Other subjects

Eurythmy

Eurythmy as a subject is part of the Steiner Waldorf school curriculum from kindergarten through to the twelfth class. It is an art of movement that is used both for education and also for artistic performance.

Eurythmy requires that we become inwardly mobile. When we hear sounds, we are taken along into continual change, from high to low, from soft to loud. We are also carried along on the course of a melody, in changes of melody and melodic moods and in the subtleties of spoken language. In eurythmy these changes and their related inner movements are made manifest by movements of the body. This is done both individually and in groups. In doing eurythmy the body becomes an instrument, visualising what otherwise is only audible, namely music and speech.

First do, then think

The awareness of one's own body is the beginning of self-knowledge. This awareness is acquired by being active, by moving. Through movement and activity children get to know their environment and become acquainted with the things around them as well as their own functioning body. In all their movements, in which they interact with their surroundings, their own body is the firm reference point.

While thinking we also move, not physically but mentally. The inner movements we make while thinking can be compared to the outer movements we make while physically exploring something. In Steiner education these two processes are continually interconnected, not just because children like to move, through which their motivation to attend school and learn is extended, but especially because learning processes backed up by movement obtain meaning. Thinking and doing are connected.

In doing eurythmy gestures we visualise the movement of the creative forces that precede language and music. We enter into the moment at which language and music are still incipient. When we sing we are able to sense this movement, while going from one tone to the next. Singing the first tone, we inwardly already move towards the following one. We then perceive how the subsequent tone must first be found; the movement toward it must be discovered before that tone can sound in tune. These are the same creative movements as the ones we visualise with our entire body in eurythmy. During the eurythmy lessons the children have, through their own movements, entered into the creative movements of language and music.

Rudolf Steiner pointed out how the creative movements we use in language and music are related to the creative forces active in nature, as well as to those that work in our physical organism. When we do eurythmy with children we address their life forces.

Moving together in a circle is an important element in kindergarten and in the first three years of the lower school. Older children will be asked to practise bringing different movements together into one entity. They no longer all walk the same form in space, but straight and curved forms.

Curative eurythmy

Curative eurythmy may be used to help a child with learning difficulties or developmental problems. Specific exercises are given to individual children to help them with their physical and inner development. This type of eurythmy is prescribed by the anthroposophical school doctor and given by a specially trained curative eurythmist.

Languages

Languages are introduced early in the kindergarten. Children are at their most receptive in the early years, and if a foreign language is brought into their daily life in some way, we help to develop their ear to take in new sounds, in the same way that it develops musically. The introduction of languages is done through the ring time with song, rhyme, finger game or circle game, or during the morning, say before an activity. The teacher or assistant needs to have a good understanding of the language, and needs to be able to pronounce it accurately, for if the children are learning from imitation, what they are imitating needs to be correct! This works in the same way as the introduction of English as a second language to those children new to English. If the staff are not familiar with any other languages, a guest, parent or specialist teacher is sometimes invited to participate in the ring time, or in a morning activity.

Television and the media

TV is embedded in our culture and taken for granted to such a degree that it is often difficult for us to question its value. Similarly, with the increasing prominence of cinema, the personal computer and video games and their adoption into everyday life, rarely is a dissenting voice heard. However, it is widely held among those involved in Steiner education, as well as by researchers in the USA, that watching TV and videos and playing computer games is detrimental to the healthy development of the child. Our reasons for this are that all children have an innate imaginative capacity and their natural state is to be active in this. This is one of the great gifts of childhood and crucial for their healthy journey into adulthood, when children acquire other faculties. As they do so, it is a capacity which is usually lost or transformed, never to be relived in the same way. TV, videos and/or computer games etc. make children unhealthily 'still' and stifle their own imaginations. By presenting the child with 'finished' images, the child is required to do no inner work (or active play) at all and their imagination is 'disabled' while watching. Afterwards, this can result in listlessness, lack of initiative and boredom; children may need to be constantly entertained. Alternatively, it may result in children being overstimulated to such an extent that they can no longer listen properly to real people – they switch on or off as they please. It is felt that this kind of stimulation is in fact *deprivation* for the child's own abundant creative abilities.

Through Steiner Waldorf education, we encourage children's natural capacity to be highly sensitive to their environment and the people around them. They are, therefore, deeply susceptible to being mesmerised; they cannot filter their absorption of the things they see and hear. We are careful in both the kindergarten and school to present material in a way appropriate to their age and sensibilities. By contrast, frequently, the quality of children's material on TV, videos and computers is very poor. They force images and noises of all kinds upon the child which are in our view inappropriate – the children may become desensitised as their threshold for violence, noise, aesthetics, moral and social behaviours – you name it – lowers. Young children do not have the discrimination to regulate their own watching. They are not yet able to know what is good for them and what is not and they depend on the adults around them to decide the boundaries, which will protect them (in all areas of life, not just this one) until they can freely take care of themselves.

Furthermore, the images that flash past on the screen are not connected to real life – they are an artificial representation of life and, as such, abstract. One cannot *relate* to TV. Children live vividly in the present and to be healthy they need to feel deeply connected to the world around them. They do not have the intellectual sophistication to cope healthily with this abstract phenomenon.

Children are discouraged from watching television or playing on computers, and if at all, only to watch on weekends.

Conclusion

We try to make our kindergartens a haven for the young child. Our unwritten motto over the door is 'Here we have time'... time for the children to experience themselves and others and grow in peace and harmony, where they feel safe and not under pressure to perform or compete, where we weave a tapestry of learning experiences for them. That is the ideal in a Steiner Waldorf kindergarten.

Appendix

Steiner Waldorf Schools Fellowship (SWSF)

The Steiner Waldorf Schools Fellowship represents Steiner or Waldorf education in the UK and Ireland. It is a registered charity and carries responsibility for advice, curriculum research, quality care and accreditation, support for legal and administrative matters, conferences, teacher training, contact with national media, international information, publishing and translating resource material, books and articles and a termly newsletter. SWSF holds the trademark on the use of the names (Rudolf) Steiner or Waldorf in the context of education.

Kidbrooke Park, Forest Row, East Sussex, RH18 5JA
Tel: 01342 822115 Fax: 01342 826004 Email: info@swsf.org.uk
Web: www.steinerwaldorf.org.uk

Accreditation

All full member and sponsored schools are registered charities regulated by the Charity Commission or relevant body. All schools and independent early years' centres are also registered with the requisite government agencies and receive inspections accordingly (from Ofsted, Estyn, HMIE etc.). Different arrangements, however, apply to schools in the Republic of Ireland. In addition to national regulations member institutions receive advisory support and accreditation through the fellowship. Full member schools seek to apply a range and depth of quality indicators included in the fellowship's code of practice and through shared good practice. 'Sponsored' schools and provisionally registered early years centres are projects developing towards full membership and receive regular accreditation visits from experienced colleagues. There are a number of small initiatives or interest groups working with elements of Steiner education or using them for home education. These are non-accredited.

Affiliate activities are similarly non-accredited. These are schools or organisations with compatible aims and objectives in mutually supportive communication with SWSF such as the European Council for Steiner Waldorf Education: www.ecswe.org. Each school is expected to implement the fellowship code of practice for administration and management.

The world list of Steiner Waldorf Schools can be found on: www.waldorfschule.info/upload/pdf/schulliste.pdf

Special educational needs

There are also a number of related, non-accredited, foundations affiliated to the fellowship. SWSF schools should be distinguished from the homes, schools and communities for children and young people in the Steiner education special schools sector. These apply an adapted Waldorf curriculum. For information:

The Association of Camphill Communities
Tel: 01653 694197 Fax: 01653 600001 Email: info@camphill.org.uk

All SWSF schools are day schools but home boarding can be arranged in some schools.

Training (early years)

A range of teacher education pathways is currently available in the Steiner Waldorf movement in Britain and Ireland. Provision includes publicly funded, privately funded, part-time, residential and full-time courses. SWSF supports courses and programmes seeking forms of public accreditation; SWSF is not an accrediting body itself.

All courses are administratively independent of SWSF. The early years courses are all part time and mostly work based. You can find direct links to them from the Steiner Waldorf Schools Fellowship website: www.steinerwaldorf.org.uk

University of Plymouth in partnership with SWSF

Foundation Degree in Steiner Waldorf Early Childhood Education
A two-year programme for early years practitioners and assistants, based in the north of England, with options for distance learning and accreditation of previous experience. Successful participants will receive a Steiner

Waldorf Early Years Foundation Degree, which will lead to Early Years Professional Status and BA.

Tel: 01395 255419 Fax: 01395 255303

London Waldorf Early Years Training Course

Three-year, part-time course held in London on Saturdays plus intensives. Teaching placement is an integral element.

Course Co-ordinator, Woodbine Cottage, Harescombe, nr Gloucester, GL4 0XD Tel: 01452 812393

Emerson College

Part-time, three-year course. Teaching practice is integrated into the programme.

Steiner Waldorf Teacher Education, Emerson College, Forest Row, Sussex, RH18 5JX Tel: 01342 822238 Fax 01342 826055

Early Childhood Education Programme

Three-year, part-time course. Foundation Year, Child Development Year, work-based Practice Year. Eight weekends (Friday evening and Saturday) and three five-day sessions each year. Teaching practice is integrated into the third year.

Raheen Wood School, Raheen Road, Tuamgraney, Scariff, County Clare, Ireland. Tel and Fax: 00 353 61 927257

Independent parenting workshops

The First Three Years – a part-time course for parent and child group leaders, playgroup leaders, parents and anyone interested in the first three years of childhood. The course consists of ten one-day workshops held in York or London. Certificates of attendance are issued. The workshops are also offered individually. Tel: 01904 612683

Affiliated organisations

The Alliance for Childhood (UK)

The Alliance for Childhood is a worldwide network of individuals and organisations committed to fostering and respecting each child's inherent right to a healthy childhood and serves as a network that facilitates reflection and action by people with concerns about the care and education of children.

It is not a conventional organisation, but an engagement in working together for the betterment of the experience of childhood. It exists in the shared work and spirit of co-operation whereby all partners can find mutual support. For information: www.allianceforchildhood.org.uk

Aims and objectives of the current partners

■ **Support family life:** The activities of the alliance promote and support family life, in all its forms, so that children grow up and develop in a secure and stable home environment.

■ **Promote a developmentally appropriate early years curriculum:** Creative play and self-directed activities give children a sound basis for lifelong learning and promote healthy emotional and social growth.

■ **Work for better physical and emotional health of children:** Parents, educators and healthcare professionals can optimise their support for children by collaborating with each other and sharing their experiences.

■ **Fight poverty and neglect in all forms:** Many children suffer poverty, neglect, abuse and discrimination, undermining the basic human right to a nurtured childhood.

■ **Question the role of electronic media in child development:** Overexposure to television, computers and video games adversely affects children's physical, emotional, social and mental development. By sharing experiences, parents and educators can work together to offer children a creative and healthy balance.

■ **Highlight the dangers of commercialism aimed at children:** Children need to be protected from the manipulation of hard selling and advertising until they are mature enough to make informed choices.

■ **Improve childcare facilities:** Parents need affordable, high quality childcare, providing a caring environment with appropriate activities for each child's developmental needs.

Bibliography and resources

Alliance for Childhood (2000) *The Future of Childhood*. Stroud: Hawthorn
      Press.
Baldwin, Dancy. R. (2006) *You Are Your Child's First Teacher*. Stroud:
      Hawthorn Press.
Ball, C.(1994) *Start Right: The Importance of Early Learning*.London: RSA.
Bettelheim, B. (1991) *The Uses of Enchantment*. London: Penguin
      Psychology Literature.
Brown, B. (1998) *Unlearning Discrimination in the Early Years.* London:
      Trentham Books.
Bruce, T. (2003) *Early Childhood Education*. Oxford: Oxford University
      Press.
Bryer, E. (2005) *Eurythmy for the Young Child (A Guide for Kindergarten
      Teachers, Eurythmists and Parents).* WECAN, Wisconsin, USA.
Carey, D. and Large, J. (2001) *Festivals, Family and Food*. Stroud:
      Hawthorn Press.
Clouder, C., Jenkinson, S., Large, M. (2001) *The Future of Childhood*.
      Forest Row, East Sussex: SWSF Publications.
DfES (2000) *Foundation Stage Curriculum*. www.dfesgov.uk
DfES (2003) *Every Child Matters: Birth to Three*. www.dfesgov.uk
DfES (2003) *Foundation Stage Parents: Partners in Learning*.
      www.dfesgov.uk
Dhom, C. (2001) *Making Magical Fairy-tale Puppets*. Fair Oaks, CA: Rudolf
      Steiner College Press USA.
Druitt, A., Fynes-Clinton, C. and Rowling, M. (1995) *All Year Round*.
      Stroud: Hawthorn Press.
Druitt A., Fynes-Clinton, C. and Rowling, M. (2004) *The Birthday Book*.
      Stroud: Hawthorn Press.
Glockler, M. and Goebel, A. (2000) *Guide to Child Health*. Edinburgh: Floris
      Press.
Grunelius,E. (1991) *Early Childhood Education and the Waldorf School
      Plan*. Spring Valley, NY: Rudolf Steiner Press. Originally published
      1952.
Jaffke, F. (2002) *Play and Work in Early Childhood*. Edinburgh: Floris
      Press.

Jenkinson, S. (1997) 'As ye sow, so shall ye reap', in *Paideia:* A Research Journal for Waldorf Education. Steiner Waldorf Schools Fellowship, **17**.

Jenkinson, S. (2002) *The Genius of Play*. Edinburgh: Hawthorn Press.

Jenkinson, S. and Rawson, M. (1998) *Educational Tasks of the Waldorf Curriculum*. Forest Row, East Susex: SWSF Publications.

Klugman, E. and Smilansky, S. (1990) *Children's Play and Learning*. new York: Teacher's College Press.

Large, M. (2002) *Set Free Childhood*. Stroud: Hawthorn Press.

Lissau, R. (1987) *Rudolf Steiner: His Life, Work, Inner Path and Social Initiatives*. Stroud: Hawthorn Press.

Male, D. (2005) *The Parent and Child Group Handbook: A Steiner/Waldorf Approach*. Stroud: Hawthorn Press.

Mellon, N. (2001) *Storytelling with Children*. Stroud: Hawthorn Press.

Molt, E. (1975) *Emil Molt and the Beginnings of the First Waldorf School*. Edinburgh: Floris Books.

Muller, B. (1987) *Painting with Children*. Edinburgh: Floris Books.

Nutbrown, C. (1999) *Threads of Thinking*. London: Paul Chapman.

Oldfield, L. (2002) *Free to Learn*. Stroud: Hawthorn Press.

Primary National Strategy Foundation Stage Toolkit. www.dfes.gov.uk

Reinckens, S. (1989) *Making Dolls*. Edinburgh: Floris Books.

Salter, J. (1992) *The Incarnating Child*. Stroud: Hawthorn Press.

Schmidt, D. and Jaffke, F. (1993) *Magic Wool Pictures*. Edinburgh: Floris Books.

Steiner, R. (1972) *A Modern Art of Education*. London: Rudolf Steiner Press.

Steiner, R. (1996a) *The Child's Changing Consciousness*. Hudson, NY: Anthroposophic Press.

Steiner, R. (1996b) *The Education of the Child*. Hudson, NY: Anthroposophic Press.

Steiner, R. (2001) *The Foundations of Human Experience (Study of Man)*. London: Rudolf Steiner Press.

Steiner, R. (2003) *Essentials of Education 1924*. Kila,Montana: Kessinger Publishing.

Steiner Waldorf Schools Fellowship (2003) *Guidelines* and *Standards and Guidance*. Forest Row, East Sussex: SWSF Publications. Tel: 01342 825005

Strauss, M. (1988) *Understanding Children's Drawings*. London: Rudolf Steiner Press.

SWSF Early Years File. www.steinerwaldorf.org.uk

Von Heydenbrand, C. (2001) *Childhood*. London: Rudolf Steiner Press.

Von Kugelgen, H. (1993) 'Fairytale Language and the Image of Man', in *An Overview of the Waldorf Kindergarten*, Vol.1. WECAN, Wisconsin, USA.
Sturrock, G. (2005), in *Nursery World*, January.

Collections and anthologies

Floris Books: Nature, Seasonal Crafts Series: 'Spring', 'Summer', 'Autumn', 'Winter', 'The Nature Corner', 'Christmas', 'Easter' etc. Edinburgh: Floris Press.
Let Us Form a Ring and Dancing as We Sing. Acorn Hill (anthologies of songs and stories). WECAN Press, USA.
Wynestones Collection: 'Spring', 'Summer', 'Autumn', 'Winter', 'Spindrift' and 'Gateways' (*Songs, Stories, Poems, Verses, Fairytales, Birthdays* etc). Stroud: Wynstones Press.

Journals and compilations

Kindling: *The Journal for Steiner Waldorf Early Childhood Care and Education*. Email: earlyearsnews@aol.com. Tel: 01223 890988
Juno: A Natural Approach to Family Life. www.junomagazine.com
A Deeper Understanding of the Waldorf Kindergarten. WECAN, Wisconsin, USA
Early Childhood: A Steiner Education Monograph (1997). Steiner Education, Forest Row, East Sussex: SWSF Publications.
An Overview of the Waldorf Kindergarten, vols 1 and 2. WECAN, Wisconsin, USA
The Young Child in the World Today. WECAN, Wisconsin, USA.

Useful websites

Floris, Hawthorn, Rudolf Steiner Press and other books available from: Booksource, 32 Finlas Street, Glasgow, G22 5DU Tel: 08702 402182 Email: orders@booksource.net
Steiner Waldorf Schools Fellowship: www.steinerwaldorf.org.uk
www.waldorfanswers.org
www.waldorflibrary.org

Resources for craft materials, toys, healthcare and Waldorf equipment

Mecurius, 6 Highfield, Kings Langley, Herts, WD4 9JT
Tel: 01923 261 646 www.mercurius-international.com

Myriad Natural Toys, The Old Stables, Nine Yews, Cranbourne, Dorset,
BH21 5PW Tel: 01725 517085 www.myriadonline.co.uk
www.waldorf-toys.com

Weleda (UK) Ltd, Heanor Road, Ilkeston, Derbyshire, DE7 8DR
Tel: 0115 944 8200 www.weleda.co.uk